READING AUGUSTINE

Cascade Companions

The Christian theological tradition provides an embarrassment of riches: from scripture to modern scholarship, we are blessed with a vast and complex theological inheritance. And yet this feast of traditional riches is too frequently inaccessible to the general reader.

The Cascade Companions series addresses the challenge by publishing books that combine academic rigor with broad appeal and readability. They aim to introduce nonspecialist readers to that vital storehouse of authors, documents, themes, histories, arguments, and movements that comprise this heritage with brief yet compelling volumes.

1. *Reading Augustine* by Jason Byassee

Forthcoming:

Theology and Culture by D. Stephen Long
An Introduction to the Desert Fathers by Jason Byassee
Dante by Joel James Shuman
1 Peter by John H. Elliot

READING AUGUSTINE
A Guide to the *Confessions*

Jason Byassee

Cascade Books
A division of *Wipf & Stock Publishers*
199 West 8th Avenue, Suite 3 • Eugene OR 97401

READING AUGUSTINE
A Guide to the *Confessions*

Cascade Companions

ISBN: 1-59752-529-4

Cataloging-in-Publication data:

Reading Augustine : a guide to the Confessions / Jason Byassee.

viii + 94 p.; 20.3 cm.

ISBN 1-59752-529-4

1. Augustine, Saint, Bishop of Hippo. Confessions.
2. Theology—History—Early Church, ca. 30-600.
I. Title. II. Series.

BR65 A62 B53 2006

Manufactured in the U.S.A.

CONTENTS

PREFACE

Augustine's *Confessions* recounts a journey undertaken with friends. This small project is, no less, the fruit of friendship. I am grateful to Kurt Berends, coordinator of the Christian Scholars Program at the University of Notre Dame for initially approaching me to write study guides on patristic texts for college fellowship groups. Kurt followed that invitation up by initiating student discussion groups at Duke University and the University of North Carolina, then taking the participants and me all out to eat to discuss the first draft of the guide and how to improve it. What author could dream of such intensive feedback? I was as nervous as I was before my dissertation defense, but as well fed as . . . I can't remember when. Kurt then also initiated discussions with Jon Stock at Wipf & Stock to make this guide and a forthcoming one on the *Sayings of the Desert Fathers* a reality. I owe enormous thanks to him, to Jon, and to my editor K. C. Hanson.

I'm grateful to Professors Lewis Ayres of Candler School of Theology and Robert Wilken of the University of Virginia for teaching me to read Augustine. Both are model scholars. My own work, as reflected by my day job at the *Christian Century*, is much more journalistic, and aimed at non-specialists. Yet if I've gotten anything right according to the scholarship it is thanks to them.

I am grateful also to three small churches in rural North Carolina. I wrote this book in the basement of the parsonage of Purley and New Hope United Methodist Churches in Blanch, where my wife was pastor from 2001–2004. At the same time I was a student pastor at Shady Grove United Methodist, also in Caswell County. My hope with this work was to bring the sort of scholarship I got in Duke's graduate program (with an occasional jaunt up to UVa) in contact with the sort of ordinary church life we treasured at these three congregations, topped off with the energy of a campus fellowship group like Intervarsity. Our churches' patience with my life as a scholar-preacher helped inspire and make this possible.

I dedicate this book to the memory of my mother, Mary Ellen Schroeder: may God's Spirit hasten her to the beatific vision.

INTRODUCTION

SAINT AUGUSTINE IS, ARGUABLY, the second most important interpreter of the Christian faith after St. Paul. His literary contribution so affected the church in the West that we scarcely recognize his fingerprints on our lives anymore. No one in the western world can even *think* in such crucial fields as the nature of God, the soul, the church, the state, or even "religion" as such without (now usually unacknowledged) reference to Augustine. If his intellectual stature is indeed this great, then we can say that his *Confessions* is the most important Christian text outside the Bible itself. For it is Augustine's greatest work, his most lasting contribution to both the church and western society more generally, the one without which even self-avowedly non-religious people would experience the world quite differently than they now do.[1] If the *Confessions* feels *familiar* to us, it is because Augustine has so deeply affected the ways we think about the world—and more importantly, about God.

---

[1] Henry Chadwick, in a very fine introduction to Augustine, nicely details the ways all of western thought and experience is affected by Augustinian categories. See his *Augustine: A Very Short Introduction* (New York: Oxford University Press, 2001).

That is not to say that *Confessions* is read as often or as deeply now as it deserves. We contemporary Christians tend to try to satisfy our spiritual and intellectual palates with such coarse fare as may be offered at the local Christian bookstore, or on the "religion" shelf at the chain book outlet, all the while neglecting the vast bounty in our own churchly heritage that would supply far more in the way of solid food for the mature. I myself write as and for "evangelicals"—not the barbarians lampooned in the media—but more properly defined as those who cherish a deep respect for scripture and hold that the gospel must be preached to the ends of the earth. I also write as and for those who hold a "catholic"[2] trust that God's presence is mediated to us through quite material means: the flesh of Christ, bread, wine, water, liturgy, scripture, and, above all, the church. For me these concerns do not conflict with one another, but rather jointly push me toward a lifelong project of helping rediscover the riches of the ancient church's heritage. Nor in these tenets am I alone. There seems to be a movement afoot among young Christians generally to draw deeply from the long-neglected wells of the "church fathers," those Christian teachers much closer in years and in thought to the world of the bible than we. You have perhaps taken up this study guide because of similar beliefs (or through coercion by others who find them amenable!). My hope is that reading *Confessions* through the lenses offered in these short pages will both deepen your evangelical and catholic instincts, and challenge them through unfamiliar teaching that will both stretch and sustain you in surprising ways. For this has been my own experience with the fathers:

[2] I use the words "evangelical" and "catholic" with lower case letters intentionally—I do not mean to signal specific institutional affiliation by them, but rather to suggest a broad sense of each word. My own Methodist heritage itself is marked by a certain "evangelical catholicity."

they have made me *more* evangelical, *more* catholic, and just so, more deeply devoted to Jesus.

What sort of book is the *Confessions*? Augustine uses the word "confession" in at least two ways in the work. Obviously he means in these pages to confess the sins of his youth, committed as he made his way through his training as a Roman rhetorician, through his years as a Manichaean heretic, to his conversion to Platonist philosophy, and finally to the Catholic Church. More importantly though, he means here to "confess" the truth of God revealed in Jesus Christ. A "confession" is finally a note of praise, both for past sins forgiven, and more importantly for God's patient, yet adamant, guiding of Augustine back from the far country of sin to his father's house. Protestants have often made the mistake of reading *Confessions* as the story of a single conversion, which comes at the end of Book VIII. Such a reading overlooks the series of several "conversions" throughout Augustine's life: one toward "philosophy," another away from Manichaeanism, and so on. Further, it ignores the fact that *Confessions* continues on well past Book VIII, into matters that seem to us esoteric, but were crucial to Augustine's mind. Other important misreadings to avoid include an overly Freudian one that sees in Augustine's mistreatment by his father and complicated relationship with his mother the true rationale for his religious and sexual angst. Such modern categories were foreign to his thought, and fail to provide sufficient explanatory insight into the text. Another misreading would be to see this as a sort of universally applicable "religious" text, one that could apply to any spiritual seeker in any culture, so that Augustine's final goal of a specifically Christian adherence then need not weigh in to our appraisal of the work. Again, such an approach to the text smacks of modern notions rather than Augustinian ones, and Augustine himself insisted that his

3

"restless heart" could only be satisfied by the quite material truth of the incarnation and the church.

Current scholarship on the *Confessions* suggests that we be attentive to the *liturgical* elements in this work, that is, those having to do with Christian worship: baptism, the Lord's Supper, preaching, scripture, and so on.[3] Augustine, at the time of this writing in the late 400s, was a preacher—a bishop of a port town in north Africa called Hippo Regius. As any good preacher is inclined to do, Augustine is here *working* on us, his hearers, trying to lure us into the truth of God, mediated as this is by the church's worship. As such there is a fiercely adamant *moral* stridency to this text. Ancient Christians did not submit to baptism if not convinced they could live genuinely holy lives. One dare not return to a life of sin after baptism, for the refusal of a grace once given was worse than never having received baptism at all.[4] Augustine himself delayed his approach to the

[3] I refer especially here to the magisterial work of James J. O'Donnell, whose three-volume commentary on *Confessions* will remain the foundational scholarly treatment on this work for generations. See O'Donnell, *Augustine: Confessions,* 3 vols. (Oxford: Clarendon, 1992). The introduction to the work in volume I would be most helpful to beginners. Much of the rest of the work requires a high degree of Latin proficiency.

[4] There was intense debate in the church before Augustine's day whether one could sin *at all* after baptism and still be saved! Generally post-baptismal sin required serious and difficult public penance to be absolved. It was only later that a complex system of confession, penance, and absolution developed in the church to respond to this problem. Notice there is in *Confessions* little sense that Augustine might sin at all after his baptism. This does not represent any foolish confidence in his own power—far from it—but rather an extraordinary confidence in God's ability to reshape life in the church, to make it holy. Later Augustine grew impatient with claims to permanent sinlessness after baptism. Robert Markus describes Augustine's insistence on the continuing struggle with sin after baptism as "a vindication of Christian mediocrity"; *The End of Ancient Christianity* (Cambridge:

baptismal font out of fear he could not remain chaste, for example. Now, on the far side of baptism and indeed from a bishop's chair, Augustine wants to convince us to do other than he did: to embrace the truth of Christ immediately, with all the moral difficulty, stridency, and indeed, joy, that such an embrace entails.

This study guide is designed to be read simultaneously with the text of *Confessions*. This has proved difficult since the key themes of the work are so tightly intertwined as to be all but impossible to examine individually. Hopefully particular themes can be examined here without the coherence of the entire work unraveling. Like any great text, *Confessions* will stretch you at points, especially toward the end. Know that masterful intellects have spent lifetimes on this work, only to begin to discover its depths after years of study. All the same, you have much from which to benefit even on a cursory first reading. The questions here are designed to guide your intellectual perusal of the text, but more importantly to shape your spiritual life in Augustinian ways. For if that does not take place, then Augustine's deepest purpose in *Confessions* has failed.

Cambridge University Press, 1990) 53.

Chapter One:

BOOK I

THERE IS A GREAT irony in the *Confessions* not often commented upon: that a Christian convinced
that "pride," that is, undue self-attention at the expense of
attention to God, is the worst of sins should tell us such
intimate details of his personal life.[1] Critics of Augustine
suggest that modern western culture's obsession with self-
ish introspection—that is, combing the depths of oneself
while neglecting others in the world outside—can be traced
to Augustine.[2] On this account there is a short step from
Augustine's *Confessions* to books by the same title on today's bookshelves with subtitles like "confessions of a video
vixen"; "confessions of an economic hit man"; and "confessions of an ugly step-sister"! Here "confession" is made as

[1] James J. O'Donnell, *Augustine: Confessions,* 3 vols. (Oxford:
Clarendon, 1992) 1:xlii.

[2] The charge that Augustine paved the way for the modern, interiorly
obsessed self (or even invented it) is common in Augustine scholarship.
Its most sophisticated proponent may be Charles Taylor in his *Sources
of the Self: The Making of Modern Identity* (Cambridge: Harvard
University Press, 1989). For a refutation of Taylor's (and other)
efforts to read Augustine as ancestral to liberal modernity, see Michael
Hanby, *Augustine and Modernity* (New York: Routledge, 2003).

salacious as possible for the sake of self-aggrandizement and economic gain. How is Augustine's work different?

Augustine's answer might be that his *Confessions* slowly move from attention to himself to attention to God—he is rarely self-referential in the work's final books.[3] In fact, Augustine is surprisingly reticent in providing information about his own life at all. If one were to string together what we learn of his life altogether, *Confessions* might only include one book rather than thirteen.[4] In fact, the bulk of *Confessions* is not about Augustine at all, but about God, or *to* God, in the form of prayer. Like the best autobiographers in the history of the church, Augustine does not seek attention to himself for his own sake, but rather he seeks to provide a model by which his readers will see their lives as similarly driven by providence to return from the loneliness of sin to the community with God and others that is divine grace.[5] Besides, what sort of autobiography works so hard to detail the author's embarrassing mistakes? In the ancient world a writer with enough means to write about himself would take pains to present his achievements and hide his missteps.

Theologian Charles Mathewes goes a step further to argue that *Confessions* is a sort of *anti-autobiography*.[6] From

---

[3] Ibid., xlix.

[4] Serge Lancel, *St. Augustine,* trans. Antonia Nevill (London: SCM, 2002) 211.

[5] A modern parallel would be the autobiographical work of Frederick Buechner; among others see his *Telling Secrets* (San Francisco: HarperSanFrancisco, 1991). Though it may be that Buechner remains mostly in the orbit of self-examination and never quite reaches for contemplation of the divine mystery that Augustine achieves in *Confessions,* Books X–XIII.

[6] See his "Book One: The Presumptuousness of Autobiography and the Paradoxes of Beginning," in *A Reader's Companion to Augustine's Confessions*, ed. Kim Paffenroth and Robert Kennedy (Louisville:

his first words Augustine is concerned not with himself, but ✓
with God. Augustine narrates his life here as a series of false
steps in self-assertion—the desire to make a place for himself in a world that respects only power, self-amusement,
wealth, and family status. He makes no mean effort toward
accumulation of those things, and precisely so drifts farther away from the God in whose presence life is most fully
lived. His is no life at all then—only after the fact of his
conversion can he narrate his missteps as false attempts to
flee a God he cannot escape. This is also no autobiography
because Augustine cannot even remember his own beginning. He has to look for evidence for what infants are like
from others. He just as certainly cannot see his own end, as
none of us can. In fact, for the Christian bishop now looking retrospectively over his life as he writes, no one can see
their end until *the* End, in which God gathers all things to
himself, judges, and appropriates everything to its eternal
place. In the meantime Augustine remains "scattered," in a
place of "disintegration," until God gathers him and us all
up and becomes all in all (Chadwick 24).[7] Augustine can
give no account of his life that does not look away from
himself and toward that eschatological horizon when he
will receive his true self—and neither can we, as *Confessions*
makes clear.

Augustine is fully aware of the presumption not only
in writing his own life's story, but in trying to address God
properly at all. We are mere creatures, God is an unchang-
ing and infinitely good creator—what words can the former
properly apply to the latter? Yet as creatures of a good God
we have been gifted by the desire to pray and praise. In that

Westminster John Knox, 2003) 7–23.

[7] This study guide will use the translation by Henry Chadwick:
Confessions, The World's Classics (Oxford: Oxford University Press,
1992). Subsequent references to Chadwick will be parenthetical.

gift we can see a mirror image of the one whom we seek, without whom we are unendingly restless, in whom we have our fullest joy (3). Augustine here wrestles with what philosophers call "epistemology"—the question of how we know what we know. For him, our desire to praise is key to our knowledge about anything. For our knowledge runs aground as it seeks after God:

> Who then are you, my God? . . . Most high, utterly good, utterly powerful, most omnipotent, most merciful and most just, deeply hidden yet most intimately present, perfection of both beauty and strength, stable and incomprehensible, immutable and yet changing all things, never new, never old, making everything new . . . ." (5)

Language itself creaks under the strain, and must resort to paradox to show that this one cannot properly be spoken about. Yet language itself stretches toward the one who is all wisdom and delight, and in our very failed efforts to speak of God we can see something of his grace. Throughout *Confessions* knowledge and love are twins, reflecting in us creatures the Wisdom and Love that are the Son and Holy Spirit within the life of God. Our attempts to know God, or anything else, are indelibly triune, if only seen in fits and starts. When we properly love and know God we catch a glimpse—insofar as creatures can—of the Mystery of the divine life. Our very desire to praise rightly is a hint at the nature of the One we desire. Fortunately for us we can do more than strain intellectually and morally after such glimpses—for the One we strain to see becomes incarnate among us, giving us far more than mere hints.

There is much we could focus upon in this and every book, and much we must leave behind. Another key theme in this first book is that of *education*. Since this series is aimed at those who have invested a great deal of time and money in their own educations, it should prove worthy of our attention. Augustine is clearly unimpressed with his early educational experiences. Not only was the teaching poor, and often accompanied by beatings, its goal was clearly the acquisition of "deceitful riches," rather than any love of learning for its own sake (11). Like any child he loved to play, and he remembers his disciplinarians as hypocrites for refusing to let the children do so, while "playing" their own games with impunity (12).[8] They paid meticulous attention paid to proper grammar and phrasing, all the while reciting licentious actions of pagan gods without shame (20). In a moment of dark humor, Augustine muses that a student would be ridiculed for mispronouncing the "h" in *homo* (Latin for "human"), but he could hate another human being with no questions asked (21). For the converted and consecrated bishop looking back on his life, both the form and content of his early education were intolerably antithetical to the love for Christ that now guides him.

For Reflection

- To what extent does *Confessions* seem to be an autobiography?

- How, and to what degree, can we know God?

- This book leads us to ask about our own educations. How were their form (the way we were taught) and content (what we were taught) helpful or a hindrance to our returning from the prodigal's far country to our father's house?[9]

---

[8] Rowan Williams brilliantly discusses the theological and moral seriousness of childhood playing in his *Lost Icons* (Edinburgh: T. & T. Clark, 2000).

[9] For example, I write as one whose education cost my family and

- In our day as in Augustine's, an expensive education is crucial to a lucrative career. For Augustine it is clear that this pursuit of social and economic advance was a detriment to his nascent spiritual life. How have you experienced anything similar?

others' some quarter of a million dollars (mostly in the form of scholarships), which has bought me the privilege of writing books like these, and being addressed as "reverend" and "doctor."

Chapter Two:

BOOK II

FOR WHOM DOES AUGUSTINE write these *Confessions*?
He is surely not informing God of anything God does
not already know. Therefore he can only be writing *for us*:
"that I and any of my readers may reflect on the great depth
from which we have to cry to you" (26). These "depths"
are summed up for Augustine in a key scriptural verse, 1
John 2:16, where lust, ambition, and *curiositas*[1]—a dis-
tracting interest in created things without reference to their
Creator—are diagnosed as a kind of malevolent trinity of
sin. Much of *Confessions* can be read as a commentary upon
the intertwining of these three in a web that catches the
young Augustine until God unravels it, and re-strings it,
so that Augustine's desire would be turned into a harp on
which to play music pleasing to God.

We have already noted Augustine's wrestling with his
ambition in the previous book. This also explains a curious
episode here in Book II—his father Patrick's pride at seeing

---

[1] I use the Latin here because the English cognate, "curiosity," is a
false one and would be somewhat misleading to use. Paul Griffiths,
a great Augustinian theologian of our day, is presently at work on a
book about *curiositas* in Augustine.

Augustine's sexual maturity in the bathhouse, a moment that tempts us moderns to armchair Freudian analysis (26–27). In point of fact, the issue at hand here is the worldly desire to see a family grow in size, wealth, and power, all of which would redound to the glory of the head of the household (and all of which is rejected by Christian asceticism, discussed below).[2] The second strand of the malevolent trinity is seen here for the first time: Augustine's struggle with lust, which he now wishes his pious mother had curbed by arranging a marriage for him (24–26). The third strand is here shown in greater detail than before: *curiositas*, a misdirected attention to trivial things for their own sake. We see it in the strange episode of the theft of the pears (28–29). He and his friends had no need of the fruit. They had far better pears available at home. They did not even put them to any use. They simply stole them because stealing is forbidden, and because they could not withstand the egging on of one another. Not only do we hear an echo of scripture's original and fruit-related sin (Genesis 3), but also Augustine's first exploration in this work of the theme of evil as a mere counterfeit good. His young "unfriendly friends" formed a society that encouraged one another in evil, in a sort of demonic parody of the church, which is meant to be a holy society of friends, encouraging each other to virtue (47).

This book is often pointed to as an example of Augustine's neuroticism, and proneness to exaggeration,

[2] For more on this see the masterful work by Peter Brown, *The Body and Society: Men, Women, and Sexual Renunciation in Early Christianity* (New York: Columbia University Press, 1988). This book helps explain what early Christians thought they were trying to accomplish through ascetic practice. The book's value is not only in Brown's sympathetic ear to ancient voices, and his unmatched prose style, but also in his ability to help us see past the polemical attack on ancient Christian sexual renunciation bequeathed to us by the Reformation, the Enlightenment, and Modernity.

over his past sin. James O'Donnell says in his recent popular biography of Augustine that if there are any titillating parts of *Confessions*, he has yet to find them![3] And sure enough, Augustine's inner tumult over his past sin seems remarkably disproportionate to the gravity of the deeds actually committed. He says of his confusion between lust and love that the "two things boiled within me. [Confusion] seized hold of my youthful weakness sweeping me through the precipitous rocks of desire to submerge me in a whirlpool of vice" (24)—would that we wrote like that!). Of his theft of the pears he remembers his exultation then with pity: "I had no motive for my wickedness except wickedness itself. It was foul, and I loved it" (29). Historian John Cavadini calls our attention to the relentless rhetorical excesses in this chapter, often involving swirling, violent motion, as in the first quote above.[4] He suggests this book is marked by an almost palpable sense of *sadness*, epitomized in its final sentence: "I became to myself a region of destitution" (34). Cavadini offers his own, more piquant translation: "I had made of myself a land of empty lack," a desolate landscape. As Augustine explores the depths of his sin, his rhetoric is appropriate, even in its very excess. For sin with no purpose, no function, no explanation, is a perfect analogy to the theft of the forbidden fruit in the garden, by which Adam and Eve gained nothing, except the very wasteland of independence from God Augustine describes here: "It was foul, and I loved it." The point is best made with a pedantic example,

[3] This from the author of the definitive modern three-volume commentator on *Confessions*! (see n. 3 above). The biography is James J. O'Donnell, *Augustine: A New Biography* (New York: HarperCollins, 2005). The biography has serious flaws unfortunately, which I describe in a review in *Books and Culture* (Sept/Oct 2005).

[4] In "Book Two: Augustine's Book of Shadows," in *A Reader's Companion to Augustine's Confessions*, ed. Paffenroth and Kennedy, 25–34.

for sin is itself an abyss, a puzzle, an act without motive, a senseless rebellion against a God who cannot finally be escaped, a wandering into a trackless waste, farther and farther from one's genuine self as one in communion with God. All the pears gained Augustine was "a few more satisfied pigs," says Cavadini—it gains us nothing more glamorous or explicable either.[5]

For Reflection

- Are you surprised at Augustine's level of horror at his past sin of stealing pears?

- Does his memory of his own pre-conversion behavior help you to reframe memory of past behavior you once thought trivial, but now may be seen with similar horror? Or is Augustine simply neurotic?!

- What do you suppose Augustine means by "curiosity"? Why would he consider this something to be avoided?

- What do you think of the description of sin and evil as a sort of lack or waste? Does it do justice to the palpable presence of evil we see in the world and in our own lives?

- Augustine looked to 1 John 2:16 as an especially important verse to reflect on his life. Is there a particular biblical passage that expresses how you have reflected on your own life?

[5] Ibid., 34.

Chapter Three:

BOOK III

IN BOOK III THE pace of the *Confessions* begins to quicken. As part of Augustine's education in Carthage, he seeks to grow in eloquence by reading the great orator Cicero's book *Hortensius* (now unfortunately lost to us) (39). We can catch a glimpse of Augustine's view of his education by thinking of how today's cynics view lawyers or politicians: as people who will speak whatever is necessary, regardless of the truth, to get their way and become wealthy. Rhetoric was of enormous *political* import in the ancient world, for those who could speak well could get their way with crowds, senators, emperors. Augustine remembers that he had been merely searching for more such lucrative tricks while reading Cicero, but instead found that the book "changed my feelings." His prayers, desires, even his very loves, were all altered through the reading of a single book. His former hopes seemed vain now, and "how I burned, how I burned with longing to leave earthly things and fly back to you" (39). We might see this as the first of several "conversions" in the *Confessions*: the conversion from uncritical worldly ambition to *philosophy*.

Augustine's ardor for Cicero's work is cooled only by the noticeable absence there of the name of Jesus, which he had loved from his infancy as he drank it in with his mother's milk (40). Turning back to the scriptures of the Catholic Church of his youth, he found them crude compared to the "dignified prose" of Cicero. So he fell in with the Manichaeans, a group that never tired of speaking of the Son of God and the Holy Spirit—they believed the latter had become incarnate in their founder Mani, as the Son had become incarnate in the man Jesus. The Manichaeans explained the brute reality of evil in the world as the result of a cosmic clash between two opposed principles: light (exemplified in the sun and moon) and darkness (seen above all in the evil of material existence). In this mythic battle some of the light has been captured, imprisoned in darkness, and can only be restored to the realm of light by proper action of the "elect" within the Manichaean community—actions such as eating cucumbers and sexual renunciation (before we Christians laugh too hard, we should remember the oddness of much of what we believe about good, evil, eating, and sex!). Much more could be said here,[1] but suffice it to say that for the retrospective-looking Augustine, the Manichaeans were principally appealing because they had an explanation for the evil in the world, for which the Catholics left him wanting. Further, the Catholics were unable to account for the anthropomorphic depiction of God in their own scriptures (describing God in human terms, as

---

[1] An excellent and approachable resource for more on this and all matter of Augustiniana is Allan D. Fitzgerald, O.S.A., editor, *Augustine Through the Ages: An Encyclopedia* (Grand Rapids: Eerdmans, 1999). An explosion of Augustine scholarship in the last few generations has made an embarrassment of riches available for all manner of scholars, from beginners to experts, to put to use. I mention here only the highlights.

having a "face" for example), and for the obvious immoralities of their own greatest biblical figures—the patriarchs.

That the Manichaeans' erudition so appealed to Augustine shows that the learning of Catholics in Roman north Africa left much to be desired (and that the appeal of esoteric eastern religions began long before the hippies of the 1960's!). Just think of Monica, whose fidelity to the church no one could doubt, but whose intellectual training in the faith is shown to be wanting several places in Confessions. In Augustine's life's work after his conversion he almost single-handedly redressed this wrong.

A final note on this book is the lovely depiction in it of Augustine's mother Monica, especially in her prayers for her son. She drew some comfort from a dream that her wayward son would return to God (49). Yet she continued to pester church leaders to work on the willful boy. A certain bishop refused even to speak with Augustine, calling him unteachable. Nevertheless, he encouraged Monica to take heart, for "it is inconceivable that he should perish, a son of tears like yours" (50–51).

For Reflection

- Have you had a book change your desires in the same way? Which one(s) and why?[2]

- Have you felt a similar passion for philosophy—that is, the "love of wisdom" (or should we say Wisdom [1 Corinthians 1:24]) that passionately drives all of life? Why or why not?

---

[2] I owe to Professor Robert Wilken (University of Virginia) the observation that Augustine's description of a single book "changing my feelings" is so deeply extraordinary that one should be grateful to have it happen once in one's life.

- What account for the origin of evil has your church made available to you? Of the immoralities of the patriarchs—such as Abraham's lies, or Jacob's trickery?

- Has the Bible's description of God as having human "parts," such as hands, or feet, or sitting upon a throne, troubled you? Why or why not? And why did these things so trouble Augustine?

- How important is education generally and in Christian faith to the task of evangelism and the retention of precociously learned church members?

- Do tears indeed make prayers more powerful? How?

- A venerable Eastern Orthodox monastic tradition speaks of tears as a sort of second baptism—washing away the sins committed since the first one. Do prayers without tears become overly glib?

- On the other hand—despite the assurance of the good bishop—isn't it possible that the son of such tears could have been lost?

Chapter Four:

BOOK IV

T HE MOST IMPRESSIVE FEATURE of this book is
Augustine's moving, and complicated, account of his
childhood friend (56–61). Though the Christian bishop
looking back can judge the friendship to have been inade-
quate, because it was not founded on the Holy Spirit's charity (Romans 5:5), nevertheless the two were beautifully dear
to one another. Augustine's friend fell deathly ill, and while
unconscious was baptized into the Catholic Church of his
family. We note here a great difference between Christian
thought of Augustine's time and most of ours: for the
church of Augustine's age, baptism *really does something*. It is
not merely a symbol of something else (a previous spiritual
conversion for example). On the contrary, baptism actually *effects change* in its recipients (1 Peter 3:21). As a result
of it, Augustine's friend not only recovers physically, he is
also changed spiritually beyond measure. When Augustine
tries to get him to join in his Manichaean mockery of the
Catholic rite, his friend recoils, "horrified at me as if I were
an enemy" (57). Augustine's church had such confidence in
baptism because in the sacrament God had promised to be
present. Therefore sick people on death's door, or infants, or

21

mentally disabled people were valid candidates for baptism, since what mattered in it was not so much the individual's spiritual or intellectual state, but the promise of God.

Augustine's friend finally does die, giving rise to one of the most eloquent expressions of human grief in all of literary history:

> "Grief darkened my heart." Everything on which I set my gaze was death. My home town became a torture to me; my father's house a strange world of unhappiness; all that I had shared with him was without him transformed into a cruel torment. My eyes looked for him everywhere, and he was not there. I hated everything because they did not have him, nor could they now tell me "look, he is on the way," as used to be the case when he was alive and absent from me. . . . Only tears were sweet to me, and in my "soul's delights" weeping had replaced my friend. (57–58)

Augustine's friend had been to him "my 'other self.' . . . 'He was half my soul.' I had felt that my soul and his soul were 'one soul in two bodies'" (59). Augustine reaches similar heights of rhetorical beauty later when describing his grief over the loss of his common-law wife (109); interestingly, like his friend here, she is also never named in *Confessions*. Yet for all this profound depth of feeling, Augustine insists the friendship was illegitimate. For he had "poured out my soul on to the sand by loving a person sure to die as if he would never die" (60). For love to be genuine it must be "channeled," so to speak, into love for the Maker of all things (63–64). People must be loved "in God," not as ends in and of themselves, if such love is to be permanent and stable rather than risky, and liable to loss.[1]

[1] Augustine writes more extensively on the difference between love

22

These musings on the instability of human life and love without reference to God lead Augustine to his first extended meditation on Christ in these pages (64). The very death that rips friends from sides, that splits souls in half, has been taken on by Christ himself and defeated. Augustine's Christology is a worthwhile topic for exploration in its own right.[2] This brief passage shows one of its chief characteristics: its use of the Old Testament to speak well about Jesus. The incarnation is here spoken of in terms of the description of a "a bridegroom from his marriage bed, he bounded like a giant to run his course" in Psalm 18. Both images, the bridegroom and the giant, suggest extraordinary energy, passion, and mirth. The latter especially signifies extraordinary power—leaping the mountains, bounding the hills, a giant running his course. Indeed one could give describe Augustine's Christology solely by using his quotations from the Psalter here in *Confessions*. For the Psalter, as Israel's hymnbook, is a supremely appropriate place from which to speak about God's supreme unification between himself and humanity in the incarnation.[3]

James Wetzel speaks of the *Confessions'* thirteen books as "thirteen tries at self-recollection and knowledge of God."[4] He does not mean to suggest the work is made

---

of someone for their own sake and love of someone "in God" in his *De Doctrina Christiana*, available as *On Christian Teaching*, trans. R. P. H. Green, The World's Classics (Oxford: Oxford University Press, 1997).

[2] A good place to start is with Brian E. Daley's article "Christology" in *Augustine through the Ages*, ed. Fitzgerald, 164–69.

[3] I present Augustine's psalm exegesis and argue theologically for the appropriateness of Christological readings of the Psalter in my *Praise Seeking Understanding* (Grand Rapids: Eerdmans, forthcoming).

[4] James Wetzel, "Book Four: The Trappings of Woe and Confession of Grief," in *A Reader's Companion to Augustine's Confessions,* ed. Paffenroth and Kennedy, 54.

of up disjointed books without cumulative effect—though there would be something to that claim. It is rather to say that the exercise of remembering past sins is also an attempt to "remember" something he could not have known at the time—that God was active in using Augustine's wayward-ness to draw him toward the divine life. The power of the language of grief in this chapter is not just because the words are pretty, it is because they're *true*—they properly suggest the pain of loving another without reference to the Creator and Redeemer of both parties, *and also* the way such love is a shadow, however remote, of proper love of God and an-other in God. That is, no matter how far creatures drift from their creator, their efforts at love still show something of the Love that calls us into being, despite creatures' ignorance or even defiance of that fact. Wetzel puts this forthrightly: "[Augustine's] view of love, it seems to me, limits the power of sin considerably (even to the point of making sin pow-erless), but not sin's misery. We are too rooted in God, in other words, really to have broken from God, but not so rooted that we can't feel like we have."[5] Neither Augustine nor any of us can flee from God successfully, but the fictive attempt to flee can make us miserable and sever us from our true selves as they are meant to be lived in God. In Book IV, Augustine's attempted fleeing from God is remembered as identical to God's pursuit of Augustine.

For Reflection

- Do we lack something in our minimalist view of the sacraments in comparison with Augustine's great confidence in them?

- Is there any danger here of treating the sacrament

[5] Ibid., 55.

as a sort of magical rite, effective simply by virtue of having been done without any need for later conversion?

- Have you ever loved like Augustine did, and so lost like he did?

- What does he mean by loving people "in God," so as not to feel this depth of loss? (No need to go Oprah here—the point is to reflect theologically on the intertwining of profound this-worldly love with love of God).

- Why do you suppose that neither his dear friend nor his concubine are ever *named* in this text?

- Feminist scholars routinely and justly attack Augustine for failing even to mention the name of his common-law wife, despite her obvious importance to him. Frederick Crosson opines that only those who were *instrumental* to his conversion are mentioned by name.[6] That leaves the question open as to why his dear friend who died here in Book IV is nameless. What do you think?

- Does Christ seem here like a salve against a brutal world, a pious escape from the grim reality that people we love may die—when Augustine would have done better to embrace the reality of human frailty as part and parcel of what it means for us to love? Or, is Augustine fundamentally *right* when he says that to offer oneself in genuine, loving friendship without the pouring out of the Holy Spirit on

---

[6] In "Book Five: The Disclosure of Hidden Providence," in *A Reader's Companion to Augustine's Confessions,* ed. Paffenroth and Kennedy, 71–87, 84.

both parties is like a pouring of one's soul into the sand?[7]

* Is it possible successfully to evade God?
  Read Psalm 139 and reflect on the psalmist's view.

[7] These questions are explored in the classic work, John Burnaby, *Amor Dei: A Study of the Religion of St. Augustine* (London: Hodder & Stoughton, 1938); and more recently Oliver O'Donovan, *The Problem of Self-Love in St. Augustine* (New Haven: Yale University Press, 1980).

Chapter Five:

BOOK V

WE SEE NOW THAT the bubble finally bursts on Augustine's allegiance to Manichaeanism. He had long been told that questions he had about the cult would be answered by a famous preacher named Faustus, but alas, when the famed man finally appeared, Augustine found him to be poorly learned (78). The Manichaeans had placed great emphasis on their ability to explain cosmic phenomena in religious terms. So when the Manichaeans proved unable to reconcile their cosmic claims with plain scientific observation of the world, and its best living teacher could do no better, Augustine had reason to be dubious. Mani had claimed to *be* the Holy Spirit after all (76); Augustine realized he could tolerate error about natural phenomena as a Catholic, but not as a Manichaean (79).

This question goes to the heart of Augustine's experience in the first half of the *Confessions*. The Christianity of his youth was clearly marked by impressive piety, such as that of his mother Monica. Yet it was not marked by impressive learning. The Manichaeans, with all their fantastic mythology, impressed the precocious Augustine supremely because they seemed more learned than the Catholics. They had better answers to Augustine's questions about the nature of God and of evil, and were willing to look at the difficulties of the Bible with a steelier eye. Augustine is a bit like an intelligent kid from a trailer park in the U.S. south who goes off to Harvard and only then discovers that Christianity is true, despite (or maybe not?) the half-baked version of it he heard from the TV preachers back home.

Augustine himself is inclined to argue that without faith, one cannot understand. That is, a posture of faith must be already be in place before we can understand the first thing about God. This is, notice, precisely backwards from typical modern ways of understanding religion. These tend to say that "knowledge" can only take one so far, up to the edge of the precipice of religious faith. Then, in an act of will, one makes a "leap of faith" across the precipice into religious belief. For Augustine, the act of faith is nothing so heroic as that—it is properly God's work, not ours. Further, "faith" and "understanding" occupy overlapping territory, if you will. They never operate without one another. The Manichaeans had failed to offer a reasonable religion with space for not knowing. Faustus cannot answer all of Augustine's questions, and so ends up with a conclusion that one must take some things on faith—as the Catholics had long maintained. So some act of "faith" is prerequisite to any form of religious knowledge at all. We might go further and say that even those who deny any sort of interest in God must trust *something* to be able to investigate anything at all. And understanding is present to some degree even in the smallest amount of faith. The two work together, and work most fulsomely when both are present to a large degree. Theology, and perhaps all knowledge generally, is always a process of "faith seeking understanding."[1]

Frederick Crosson offers some suggestive hints about the structure of *Confessions* in an essay about this fifth book. He notes that Books III–VIII all end with observations from philosophers with whom Augustine is wrestling. Though the most famous of these are the Platonists of Book VII, Augustine's wrestling here with various "academic" skeptics—those who held it most safe to avoid any sort of committal belief at all. Interestingly, it is precisely at the moment he has chosen to doubt everything that he returns self-consciously to his status as a catechumen of the Catholic Church—a place where both doubt and trust can coincide on the way to genuine knowledge. Crosson also observes that the three-fold sins of 1 John 2:16—lust, *curiositas*, and ambition, are on full display in the books before and after this one. Book II demonstrates Augustine's physical lust, III his intense observation of Carthage's boiling cauldron and of the coliseum, his ambition in IV with regard to his career. Then, in the three books after V, these three sins are respectively undone in the same order as Augustine undergoes his slow conversion to Christ.

These structural observations lead to some larger questions. Historians often dispute Augustine's ordering of events. They point to the obvious fact that Augustine is no unbiased observer of his own life. Naturally he wishes to highlight certain events (say, his conversion away from Manichaeanism) and strangely avoids certain others (his present status as a bishop, for example).[2] It is well always

---

[1] This description of theology as "faith seeking understanding" is generally associated with Anselm of Canterbury in the middle ages; but it is thoroughly Augustinian—as Anselm himself knew.

[2] Paula Fredriksen lodges these complaints against Augustine and his predecessor autobiographer, St. Paul, in "Paul and Augustine: Conversion Narratives, Orthodox Traditions, and the Retrospective

to remember that this is a retrospective work being done by a Christian bishop years after the fact, for whom there is no surprise at how the narrative will turn out. Yet this is not an arbitrary imposition of meaning, if Augustine should at least get a vote on the meaning of his own life. Further, Christians are those who look for patterns in events because they hold to doctrines of creation and providence that suggest their genuine Author is no human agent at all. These *Confessions* are meant to have a co-hortative effect, or an evangelical one, if you like. Augustine is not merely waxing nostalgic here, nor trying to rewrite history for some political end. He is spotting glimpses of God's guidance throughout his life in hopes that others will see the same God and worship accordingly. One could press further and argue that the effort to find a coherent story, a plot driving toward a conclusion, is itself rooted in Jewish and Christian notions of the meaningfulness of history and of human ability to discern it and organize it into stories.

For Reflection

- Augustine raises questions for us regarding the relationship between our faith and scientific observation. How can scientific views of the world help or hinder Christian faith?

- Does Augustine here show any *fear* of observation of the natural world?

- Augustine begins tentatively to embrace Christianity in this book only after learning from Ambrose that

Self," *Journal of Theological Studies* 37 (1986) 3–34. James O'Donnell's recent biography points to more malicious motives in what he takes to be intentional acts of fraudulent self-presentation in his recent autobiography.

the faith is intellectually respectable (88–89)—how can a particularly Christian erudition further the church's evangelistic outreach?

* For all of Augustine's mistrust of education, noted above, is it not crucial to the preaching and living of the gospel in the church? Or closer to home—to the writing and reading of such a glorious work as the *Confessions*?

* How does Augustine conceive of the relationship between what he knows as "science" and what he knows as "faith"? How should we?[3]

* Does Augustine come off as a trustworthy narrator of these events? Why or why not?

* Compare the depiction of the two bishops in this book—Faustus and Ambrose. (Hint: push past the superficial reading—that Faustus is the bad one and Ambrose the good one whose religion wins Augustine over, and ask how Augustine thinks God uses each one).

[3] The relationship between science and theology is enormously complicated and no less enormously fascinating, as public debates about Intelligent Design in the US in 2005–2006 made clear. The recent three-volume work by Alister McGrath is a good place to start exploring these matters: see his *A Scientific Theology* (Grand Rapids: Eerdmans, 2001–2003). Another scholarly resource on these questions is the work of John Polkinghorne, an astrophysicist and Anglican priest. For example, see his *Exploring Reality: The Intertwining of Science and Religion* (New Haven: Yale University Press, 2006).

Chapter Six:
BOOK VI

THIS BOOK CONTAINS CHARMING portraits of several of Augustine's important soul mates.[1] We see his mother comforting salty sailors rendered pitiful because of a storm at sea—a surprising inversion of ancient expectations of gender roles on Christian grounds (90). We see Augustine's earnest efforts to approach a desired mentor in Ambrose rebuffed, and Augustine amazed that the bishop can read without speaking aloud—a rarity in an ancient reading culture that omitted spaces between all letters so as to save on expensive paper, such that printed words normally had to be read aloud to be understood (92–93).

TheLordismyshepherdIshallnotwant.(Psalm23:1).

We see Augustine's jealousy of a drunkenly happy beggar, whose livelihood from greeting strangers is surely to be preferred to Augustine the imperial rhetorician's lying to flatter

[1] Eric Plumer writes that he uses Book VI to introduce *Confessions* to his undergraduate students, since its gripping depiction of characters and events is the most likely book to lure in today's young readers. "Book Six: Major Characters and Memorable Incidents," in *A Reader's Companion to Augustine's Confessions,* ed. Paffenroth and Kennedy, 89–105.

the emperor (97–98). We see Alypius dragged against his will to the circus, only slowly giving in to the *curiositas* of butchery below and spectatorial madness above (100–101). We see Augustine's inability to be free from lust, and even his unwitting enticement of his friend's *curiositas* to draw him too toward unchastity (106–7). Finally, we see his moving portrait of the loss of his common-law wife, torn from his side, leaving him bleeding (109). Though he faults his lust, there was clearly genuine love in that relationship, ruthlessly sacrificed to his mother's ambition.

One interpreter reads Monica and Ambrose here as spiritual mother and father to Augustine.[2] Yet clearly Monica's depiction is not all positive. She arranges Augustine's marriage for his social progress, not for any more virtuous Christian rationale. Her ready acceptance of the things of Christian faith is a marked contrast to Augustine's heady reason. She can even claim to be able to distinguish true from false visions by a certain physical smell (108)! Perhaps her strongest point of contrast to her son is that she can readily give up what is for her a salutary Christian practice—feasting at the martyrs' tombs—at Ambrose's command (92). Augustine cannot bring himself to give up far less salutary practices he knows to be harmful.

The conversation with Ambrose presents a striking contrast to Faustus, the Manichaean bishop. For the Manichaeans, the highest forms of knowledge are secret, presented only to the initiate after years of preparation.[3] In

[2] I am heavily dependent on Plumer for the next few paragraphs.

[3] Though in fairness it should be said that Christian initiation—baptism—was still in Augustine's time a prerequisite for the highest "knowledge" of the Christian faith, admittance to the sacrament of the eucharist. Yet this Christian knowledge was not a form of *esoterica*, revealed in ever more elaborate and ridiculous forms of knowledge (Augustine mocks these at length in his writings against the Manichaeans, such as his repeated charge that the Manichaean

contrast, Ambrose has nothing to say to Augustine other than what he says publicly to the whole congregation in his preaching. Further, Augustine's known allegiance to the Manichaeans may have been precisely what kept Ambrose reading instead of mixing with this known heretic! Or, perhaps, Augustine is glad to be ignored, for he could receive the sort of secret that would force him to be as celibate as Ambrose.

The beggar in this book amply shows the silliness of Augustine's ambition as a rhetorician. "He had no worries, I was frenetic. . . . Yet if he asked whether I would prefer to be a beggar like that man or the kind of person I then was, I would have chosen to be myself, a bundle of anxieties and fears" (97). If anything, the beggar's way of life is to be preferred to Augustine's, whose smooth and ingratiating words to those in power did not even bring him the happiness this man receives from a bottle.

Finally, Alypius is presented in so many episodes in this book that some Augustine scholars have posited these stories originally came from another work—perhaps a sort of *Confessions* of Alypius's own. At the time of Augustine's composition, Alypius is a well-known and urbane bishop of the church. Back then the pressure of his friends could lure him into the bloodsport of the theater, even against his will. Clearly this incident is intended as a sort of negative image of the kind of friendship that would inspire us to virtuous deeds in the church (100). It is also an image of the fall—titillation, temptation, and giving in—for some-

---

elect eat animal and human ejacula). Rather, Christianity is shown to be most rational precisely in its deepest mystery—or so one might reply to the charge that Catholics are not less devoted to secrecy than the Manichaeans. For more on Catholic liturgical practice around baptismal preparation and the sacrament see William Harmless, *Augustine and the Catechumenate* (Collegeville, Minn.: Liturgical, 1995).

thing pitiful, an apple, a theatrical spectacle. This image, or echo, of Adam's fall in the garden suggests something of the way Augustine views history. Tellings of scripture's stories are meant to evoke echoes, imitations, of virtuous deeds and avoidance of sins. Said more strongly, the patterns of scripture are unendingly repeated in human life, both in our sin and our grace, and Christians ought to have eyes to see this. Yet sin and grace are not equal partners in these depictions. Sin is shown here to be patently ridiculous; grace is obviously the more beautiful of the two ways of life. The friends dragging Alypius to the stadium represent a parody of the genuine role of faithful friends to help their fellows to love God and fulfill their deepest desires by worshipping in God's church.

This is as good a time as any to discuss a theme that runs throughout *Confessions*—Augustine's struggle to find an adequate rationale for the evil in the world, for the nature of God, and for the immoralities described in the bible. These are all (loosely) of a piece for him. Augustine is glad to learn from Ambrose that the Catholic belief that humans are created in the "image of God" does not mean God is a body. Glad as he is that Catholicism is more intelligent than he thought, he is left in a pickle. For he cannot imagine what "God" can *be*, because he cannot see how a thing can be non-physical and yet exist (93–94). He is also gradually coming to see that evil is not a "thing," but a certain sort of *absence*. To use some favorite metaphors, evil is like a shirt with a hole in it—a lack that destroys the good thing; or blindness—an absence of ability.[4]

This does not mean there is no evil—far from it, Augustine has long been seeking a philosophy that can account for evil's dogged persistence. It is rather to say that

[4] The metaphors, like the description of evil as non-being, come from Platonist philosophical precedents.

there is no *thing* that is purely evil, evil is a sort of shadow, a cancer against the goodness of being that God has created. This is why even quite evil things have good aspects: the pears he once stole were beautiful; a murderer acts only out of misguided self-interest; Augustine's love for his concubine and childhood friend was genuine, if flawed. Evil is merely a parody of the good, not a principle opposed to it—you cannot go and pick up a handful of sheer evil. Augustine has also now come to see that the Catholics were more honest than the Manichaeans. They did not pretend to know everything, but rather let scripture open them to a mystery they could not conceive, that they could indeed make mistakes about, but that loved them first, and was guiding them toward truth (95–96). The rigorous pursuit of God is gradually gaining on the wayward Augustine.

For Reflection

- What do you think of Augustine's intellectual struggles in this chapter and throughout *Confessions*?

- Do his intellectual struggles lead you to wonder in similar ways about the nature of God? Of evil? Or of Christian scripture?

- Why do you think Augustine worried so much about these problems? What do you think of his solutions?

Chapter Seven:
BOOK VII

I AM OCCASIONALLY TEMPTED TO describe the
Confessions' account of Augustine's "conversion" as several gradual shifts from less to more satisfying philosophical descriptions of God and the world, though such a view
of conversion may sound oddly non-religious to our ears.[1]
Augustine continues to be unable to think of God as anything other than a material "thing," such as, perhaps, a thin
film present in all of reality (112). He continues to worry
about evil, and is curious about astrology as another poten-
tially satisfying account of its persistence in the world (117–
18). These two and other problems are solved for him only
after reading some "books of the Platonists"—how scholars
wish they knew which ones (121)! He uses the language of
conversion to describe a growing awareness of a non-mate-
rial divine nature (123). A thing can indeed *exist* that is not

---

[1] For more on "religion" as a contemporary invention see Nicholas
Lash's *The Beginning and the End of Religion* (Cambridge: Cambridge
University Press, 1996). He argues that it was only in recent centuries
that Christians have come to think of "religion" as a certain sort of
interior feeling, freely chosen by an individual, in isolation from
politics, art, science, law, economics, or to speak more theologically,
of the mystery of God and all God has created.

material, indeed Moses heard God say that "I am that I am."
If God exists in a supreme sense, then it is *creatures*, we,
that have to worry whether we exist![2] We *are* real in that we
come from the really real (God), but we *are not* real insofar
as we are not what God is. What Augustine has stumbled
upon here is a concept of *participation*. God alone truly *exists*. Creatures only "exist" by a gracious act of creation in
which God freely chooses to have other beings pass from
non-existence to existence as a reflection of his own Being.
Evil then is a kind of slide away from God and toward non-
being, but insofar as anything exists, it participates in being,
and just so is also good and beautiful. For Augustine such
a philosophical account of God and the created order was
clearly part and parcel of his conversion to Christianity.[3]

But it was not all he needed. He did not find in the
Platonist books anything like a Christian description of humility. He could find there that "in the beginning was the
Word" of John 1:1, but not that the Word was made flesh,
and dwelt among us, as in John 1:14 (121). He could find
a divine Son in the form of God, but not that Son's descent
into our world to die and rise for us (Philippians 2:1-11).
Though the Platonists had enabled him to gaze on the real,

[2] Professor Stanley Hauerwas (Duke University) uses this as an
aphoristic way to describe Thomas Aquinas' thought; but I think it
fits here.

[3] For a masterful contemporary account of these philosophical themes
see David Bentley Hart, *The Beauty of the Infinite* (Grand Rapids:
Eerdmans, 2003). John Milbank has also made it part of his Radical
Orthodoxy project to reestablish the unity of the transcendentals after
the collapse of modernism. See his *Theology and Social Theory* (Oxford:
Blackwell's, 1990), *The Word Made Strange* (Oxford: Blackwell, 1997)
and now *Being Reconciled* (London: Routledge, 2003). For a critic of
Augustine's fusion of Platonist philosophy and scriptural Christianity,
see Phillip Cary, "Book Seven: Inner Vision as the Goal of Augustine's
Life," in *A Reader's Companion to Augustine's Confessions*, ed. Paffenroth
and Kennedy, 107–26.

unchangeable truth that is eternal, he could not sustain this gaze. Though he knew to whom he must cling to see God continually—Christ—he knew he could not even cling by himself. The answer for him to these multiple problems is the incarnation: the divine humility by which God does not ask us to ascend to him of our own strength, but descends to us out of his mercy, to carry us to him. Christians are not then to look up at the one so dazzlingly high above them, but down at the God crucified at their feet (128). Though he had begun to grasp the truth of the Word (or *logos*) of God with his intellect, he as yet knew nothing of the charity, or love (*caritas*) by which the Holy Spirit binds people in humble love of God and neighbor.

A corollary of this distinction between what can be known about God philosophically and what only through the incarnation is that the latter is a participatory knowledge. That is, he could not learn of the God of Jesus simply by reading of him in books, but only liturgically: "[I] heard as it were your voice from on high: 'I am the food of the fully grown; grow and you will feed on me. And you will not change me into you like the food your flesh eats, but you will be changed into me'" (124). The Platonists could show him much about the nature of God and the perverse absence of evil, but not enough about the specifically Christian God, nor the incarnation of the divine Son to save humanity. The former knowledge without the latter would finally have been useless.

Augustine seeks to do here what Christians have always sought to do when speaking of God's relationship to creation. God must be thought of as distinct from creation. God is not a being among other beings in the world, even one diffused throughout space, or else God would be a mere creature. God is also not simply to be identified with creation, else there would be "more" of God in an elephant than a sparrow—clearly an absurd proposition (112). The difference between God and creation is not a spatial difference, as though God is far away—Augustine is clear throughout *Confessions* that God is "nearer" to each of us than we are to ourselves. Rather, the distinction between God and creation is necessary simply because creation comes from God and is radically dependent on God every moment for its existence. God must be different from something God makes out of scratch, *ex nihilo*, "from nothing," as western theologians have always said. Think of Augustine's descriptions of God as immutable and incorruptible and so on as glosses on this Christian description of God as "other" than creation. Yet that claim is not sufficient by itself. God is not only other than creation, but is also its *creator*. That is, creation has in some sense to be appropriate to the God who creates it. Otherwise it would be an arbitrary thing, without "fingerprints" from the one who cobbled it together. In more Trinitarian moods, Christians have said that it is supremely "fitting" for a God who pours out everything he is in begetting the Son, which two pour themselves out in the giving of the Spirit, can be thought of as appropriately creating a good world. Not by necessity—God is supremely free. But out of sheer goodness, as a gift that reflects something of the nature of its giver. Creation bears marks of its Trinitarian provenance for those with eyes to see.

All this reflection sounds fairly distant and philosophical. Some criticize Augustine for his heavy drawing on Platonic philosophical ideas in this portion of his thought. But look at the heavily *affective* nature of the language Augustine employs here in Book VII. "By the Platonic books I was admonished to return into myself. . . . I entered and with my soul's eye, such as it was, saw my mind—not the light of every day, obvious to anyone, nor a larger version of the same kind which would, as it were, have given out a much brighter light and filled everything with its magnitude. It was not that light, but a different thing, utterly different from all our kinds of light" (123). God is, indeed, other. "It transcended my mind, not in the way that oil floats on water, nor as heaven is above earth. It was superior because it made me, and I was inferior because I was made by it."

Yet it must be appropriate that God has made this good world, and can be seen in it, by fits and starts. This is no dry "God of the philosophers," but the benevolent creator whose joy it is to create, who gives his creatures the capacity to contemplate him and so to catch the reverberation of his own joy in creation.[4] So the effort to turn toward his own soul for glimpses of this God are not so much philosophical naval gazing—Augustine is adamant in this chapter that the fullness of what is to be known about God only comes from outside of us (*extra nos*) via the incarnation. Yet he can look to his soul for *some* truth, however fleeting, since God is creator of the soul, and of every other thing in existence. Whatever Platonist themes have here been seamlessly woven into biblical and theological speech in a way that their disjunction was not even thinkable in the church until recently.[5]

---

[4] The Platonists themselves knew no dry "God of the philosophers," as there is also a rich mystical Platonist tradition that precedes Christianity. Christians avidly learned from this for their own mystical purposes. For more on the history of Christian mysticism see Bernard McGinn's now four-volume *Presence of God: A History of Western Christian Mysticism* (New York: Herder & Herder, 1994, 1996, 1998, 2005), or more managably, Olivier Clement's *The Roots of Christian Mysticism* (Hyde Park, N.Y.: New City, 1996).

[5] This is not to say that Platonic philosophy is essential to Christian theology such that the latter would be ruined without the former. Robert Jenson has structured a fascinating systematic theology around a quite different set of metaphysical commitments. See his two-volume *Systematic Theology* (New York: Oxford University Press, 1997, 1999).

For Reflection

- Augustine discusses here what soured him on two rival religions—Manichaeanism and astrology. The former, he says, could not respond to the criticism of his friend Nebridius. If there were an attack in the spirit realm against God, why would God fight back? If he should fear injury he is not truly God (113). In response to astrology, twins born at almost the same moment often have extraordinarily divergent fates (117). What do you make of these puncturings of rival worldviews?

- What do you make of the height at which Augustine set the bar of philosophical speculation before he was able to embrace Christian truth?

- Do you know others who have made similarly philosophical turns to Christianity?

- Say more about what "Platonism" seems to have lacked for Augustine. Does it not have a surprisingly great deal to say that is completely *right*?

- Is Platonism without Christianity as dead as, say, faith without works according to St. James (James 2:14-26)? Or is Platonist philosophy as necessary to Christian teaching as, say, the Old Testament is to the New?

- Can Augustine really have learned so much Christian thought from elsewhere than the church or the scriptures—namely from "the Platonists"?

- How should Christians speak of "truth" that originates from other sources than Christianity?

- What can we learn about God from looking into our own souls?

- How does the Eucharist reverse the normal process of digestion and change us into the body of Christ, rather than our stomachs changing its substance into our bodies?[6]

---

[6] A typical Augustinian answer might be, "I don't know"—in one of his most famous quotes he says, "If you understand it, it is not God." This lack of knowledge wouldn't worry him. Who can say how God created the world? Or how God redeems us in Christ? Yet we do not simply fall silent, we can speak better rather than worse about these mysteries in ways that accord with scripture and increase our love. But any answer that becomes an easy "formula" that allows us to think we have grasped God would worry Augustine.

Chapter Eight:

BOOK VIII

In book VIII, Augustine's difficulties with Christianity shift away from the predominantly intellectual to mostly the moral sphere. He is now convinced of the truth of Catholic teaching about God and the world, but unsure whether he can submit to the difficult way of life that Christian teaching demands. In his own words, "I was attracted to the way, the Saviour himself, but was still reluctant to go along its narrow paths" (133). This particular problem is the primary significance of the story about the conversion of Marius Victorinus. Augustine's pride—his tendency to the sin described in 1 John 2:16 as "ambition"—is now gone (133–34). Yet he has still not submitted to the humble yoke of the church. He has not deigned to embrace the charity of God in the humble form of participation in the life of a people not entirely intellectually or socially respected in the world of his day (as Augustine's memories of the poorly learned Christianity back in north Africa make clear). Marius, however, does just that, and with a voice at least as proud as that with which he taught rhetoric in the hallowed political halls of the empire (136–37). Augustine now has an example before him. Not only can pride (or *curiositas*, or lust) be intellectually decided against, but another way of life can be embraced, as his model, Marius, shows.

Before moving on, we must pause over Marius's marvelous question to his friend Simplicianus. He told him he was really already a Christian. Simplicianus responded with incredulity and promised to continue to doubt him until he appeared in an actual church. Marius's reply: "'It's the walls that make Christians then?'" (136).

Augustine now has a powerful exemplar of one able (or perhaps *enabled?*) to leave behind ambition for the waters of baptism. Where will he find such enabling himself, to overcome the strong pull of lust on him? (141–42). As it happened a prominent man named Ponticianus came to visit Augustine and his friend Alypius, spotted a copy of St. Paul's letters (whole Bibles were rarely bound together in those days),[1] and told them he was a baptized Christian and avid praying person. When Augustine says he is passionately committed to the study of Christian scripture, Ponticianus tells him of the famous ascetic St. Anthony, who left behind wealth and ambition and family to live as a monk in the deserts of Egypt (142). He also tells him of two imperial

---

[1] In fact, opening the biblical text at random was not even possible until the invention of new technology in the form of a codex—a volume not unlike today's books. Before that invention one would have had to open a scroll to precisely the place desired. Leo Ferrari argues that the random choice of the verse from Romans is meant to wow an audience unaccustomed to such wonders. The extent of his argument, and its patronizing tone toward ancient persons, go a bit too far. See Ferrari, "Book Eight: Science and the Fictional Conversion Scene," in *A Reader's Companion to Augustine's Confessions,* ed. Paffenroth and Kennedy, 127–36.

officials who, upon reading about Anthony, dedicated their lives to becoming "friends of God," left their posts of power, their possessions, and their plans to marry, and became ascetics—people who vow to follow a life of poverty, chastity, and scriptural simplicity (143–44). *Now* Augustine has a model, or several, of people not only convinced of the truth of Christianity, and able to leave behind ambition, but able to leave behind lust as well.

Later Augustine's readiness to entrust himself to a life of chastity is strengthened by a strange visit from a certain "lady Continence," who not accidentally, is charming and alluring, wishing Augustine to "embrace" her, demonstrating to him that life with her is itself fruitful in its own way (151). Augustine's two wills continue to wrestle, but the one inclined to chastity is beginning to win, at least to the point that he can pray, in a justly famous line, "grant me chastity and continence, but not yet" (145)!

These events open important questions. Augustine is often spoken of as obsessed with sex in these pages, and so perhaps as an originator of the Roman Catholic Church's (and Christianity's more generally) two-millennium-long obsession with sex. Yet that can hardly be a fair description of a man who was keenly faithful to a common law wife, then has only one other sexual partner after her while awaiting an arranged marriage. Elsewhere in *Confessions* and in other important works Augustine eloquently defends the goodness of marriage against other early Christians, like Jerome, more inclined to denigrate it entirely.[2] It is clear, however, that Christianity and chastity are almost synony-

---

[2] His "The Excellence of Marriage" is available in *Marriage and Virginity*, trans. Ray Kearney, vol. I/9 of the *Works of Saint Augustine*, ed. John Rotelle, OSA (Hyde Park, N.Y.: New City, 1999) 33–61. In its patristic context this is a strongly affirmative vision of marriage and sex.

mous here for Augustine—that he, at least, was not to become a Christian without also following lady Continence.

Finally we have the famous conversion scene in the garden, another place meant to evoke a specifically biblical echo of another Garden of immense importance (Genesis 3). Conversion is a sort of undoing of the fall, or rather a participation in God's gradual undoing of the fall that *is* the church. Augustine, now convinced that the three-ringed sin of 1 John 2:16 need no longer hold him from submitting to the yoke of a life whose view of the world he finds intellectually satisfying, retreats to a garden to let his two "wills" finish their battle (see Romans 7). His landing under a fig tree brings to mind echoes of his and his friends' sin of gratuitous theft of pears in another garden years before. In this new garden, Augustine hears a child singing, "pick up and read," and remembering St. Anthony's doing the same, he grabs his copy of Paul's letters, and lands on Romans 13:13-14, "not in dissipation and drunkenness, nor in debauchery and lewdness, nor in arguing and jealousy; but put on the Lord Jesus Christ, and make no provision for the flesh or the gratification of your desires" (152–53). Here we have another conversion, perhaps the most important thus far: "it was as if a light of relief from all anxiety flooded my heart. All the shadows of doubt were dispelled" (153).

For Reflection

- What do you think of Augustine's depiction of sex in this book?

- How is our sexuality related to our following of Christ?

- Is there not a certain rather rigorous *asceticism*, that is, a training of our sexual instincts, required for

Christians whether they do marry or remain single?

- How do our rigorous ascetic demands to remain "faithful in marriage, celibate in singleness"[3] relate to the difficult ascetic demands placed on Christians in Augustine's day?

- Is it the walls that make a Christian? Must a Christian physically present her or himself to the church for baptism, the Lord's Supper, and membership? What does Marius think? What does Augustine think? And what do you think and why?

- Why should Romans 13:13-14, at that moment, bring about such a monumental change? Do you know of any similar conversion, perhaps brought on by a more elegant passage of scripture than the one that proved pivotal to Augustine? Does it shed light on the question to know that biblical language of "putting on" Christ has long been read as a reference to baptism?

- Augustine's conversion, like St. Paul's and St. Anthony's before him, has been the paradigm for countless subsequent conversions in western history and literature. St. Francis's and Martin Luther's are just two of the more famous of these. Can you think of others?

- How is it that conversion is both highly personal,

[3] The phrase is one that has taken on the status of church law in my own Methodist denomination in the context of arguments about homosexuality. Yet I think it aptly describes the rigorous demands made on most Christians, except for vowed priests and religious in Catholic or Orthodox contexts (whose demands are obviously even stricter).

and accords roughly with a well-worn script in western Christianity?

- Does this conversion, coupled with the several others throughout *Confessions*, shed light on the *genre* of this book? Is this literature intended to generate imitation of Augustine as an exemplar?

- Can *Confessions* be seen as an interpretation, an extended exegesis, of the prodigal son story?

Chapter Nine:
BOOK IX

IT HAS OFTEN PUZZLED readers why *Confessions* does not conclude with Augustine's conversion. Indeed, the anticlimactic and perfunctory description of baptism here in Book IX raises the question of why the book continues at all here. Various scholars have offered a variety of hypotheses: Augustine continues on to cover baptism, the church, death and rebirth, Christian life in the world, a critique of pagan philosophies, etc.[1] Another could be offered: Augustine finally here rests in an understanding of Christian scripture that will guide him the rest of his days. It is no longer the sorry counterpart to Cicero's elegant prose—it is a Christian

---

[1] These possibilities are catalogued in Kim Paffenroth, "Book Nine: The Emotional Heart of the *Confessions*," in *A Reader's Companion to Augustine's Confessions,* ed. Paffenroth and Kennedy, 137–54. Like almost every author in that volume Paffenroth argues that his assigned book of *Confessions* is the most important! For Paffenroth, Augustine uses the conversion scene in Book VIII to show that Platonism's aversion to things bodily and material is overcome: the beauty of this garden is no hindrance to Augustine's conversion, but a furtherance of it. In Book IX Augustine's tears at the death of his mother fly in the face of ancient Stoicism, for which such tears would simply be silly. Christianity gives an appropriate place to grief, among other "emotions."

reader's way into the divine life itself. Scripture is almost a sacrament for Augustine, whose effect on him is nothing short of ecstasy.[2] "My God, how I cried to you when I read the Psalms of David," he cries. "Songs of faith, utterances of devotion which allow no pride of spirit to enter in! . . . How they kindled my love for you! I was fired by an enthusiasm to recite them, were it possible, to the entire world in protest against the pride of the human race" (160). Augustine preached on the psalms every morning as bishop. His biographer Possidius tells us that in his last days he had the penitential psalms written and attached to the wall by his deathbed for him to read, weeping, in preparation for judgment. Clearly Augustine understands scripture not as a mere historical record of Israel and the church. It is almost a *living* document for him, through which Christ himself can grab a reader and reorient her dramatically, giving her new loves, or even a new Lord.

Confessions does not end with Book VIII, just as Christians' lives usually do not end at conversion, but rather begin there, on the way to further conversions and fuller life. Augustine's self-remembrance continues with attention to matters both great (fear of slipping back into ambition—156) and small (gratitude at the miraculous healing of a toothache, 163—though perhaps this would be no small feat for the sufferer!). We see here too the beginning of a sort of philosophical society—Augustine, his son Adeodatus, Alypius, Nebridius, and Monica, living together at Cassiciacum, conversing in the sweetness of the Spirit

[2] Augustine lived long before the church codified the number of sacraments into seven (for Catholics) and two (for Protestants)—any site where humans might meet God's saving work is a sacrament for Augustine, including the reading of scripture. See the article by Emmanuel J. Cutrone, "Sacraments," in *Augustine through the Ages: An Encyclopedia*, ed. Alan D. Fitzgerald (Grand Rapids: Eerdmans, 1999).

about the things of God. Quite a change from the society of friends of Augustine's early days in Book II.

This would be an appropriate time to pause over the place of Monica in the story of the *Confessions*. This pious woman had enrolled her small son in the list of those to be baptized (catechumens—literally "those being taught") early in his life, though the adult Augustine, writing after the fact, sharply disagreed with her logic for delaying baptism at that time (13–14). She had planted a love for the name of Jesus in his heart by singing to him from an early age, and yet she cherished ambition of her intelligent son's great success in the world, and refused to quell his lust by finding him a wife. If he was in the heart of Babylon, Augustine writes, Monica was in the outskirts of the city (28). Later Augustine had to lie to his mother to escape her clutches and sail for Europe. God acted in her best interests there since Augustine's ship took him eventually to Milan and St. Ambrose's influence. Clearly the "smother love" Monica practiced is not necessarily godly![3] Though there was much of the "old Eve" left in her, though she was still "too carnal," allowing and indeed encouraging Augustine's ambition and lust, nevertheless her tears would prove the flood that bore him into the font of baptism (81–82). Here in Book IX we get the most fulsome picture of Monica, as an early wine sipper (if not swiller!—167), as one who bore with a husband's infidelity and won his mother to the faith (169), whose Christianity kept her from gossip and led her husband properly to beat the servants (!) (169). She would positively pester bishops (50–51), and yet gleefully submitted to Ambrose's prohibition of celebrating the martyrs' feast days (his fear was excessive drunkenness and gluttony) out of deep reverence for him personally (91–92). Monica

[3] I take the terrific description "smother love" from Professor Philip Cary (Eastern College).

cuts an odd figure across these pages. Her influence is enormous, but not always positive. Her piety is undoubted, if a little ill-informed. Her love for her son is patent, if not a little overbearing. And now we have Augustine's most profound reflection on his mother's role in his life (170–72). In conversation with his mother, while at Ostia overlooking the Tiber River, Augustine and she experienced *together* the final spiritual ascent described in *Confessions*. This one is not marked by the disappointment of inability to sustain that we saw in Book VII, nor by the solitary nature of each previous ascent. Here Augustine and his mother together, in conversation about eternal life, lift their minds' eyes toward God and just brush up against eternity with their hearts (171). Augustine has come to see contemplation as not simply a solitary spiritual accomplishment for a few elite, but rather a joint venture, one that an educated rhetorician and his pious but uneducated mother can undertake together. The rest of Augustine's career will be marked by an effort to help Christians like both him and his mother achieve this common goal while sustaining a life of charity between them in the church.

Monica helps bring about one more significant convert besides Augustine: "At the end when her husband had reached the end of his life in time, she succeeded in gaining him for you" (170). Augustine even makes some conciliatory comments about his enemies, the Manichaeans, here: "But then my pity for them returned because they were ignorant of your remedies, the sacraments" (160). It is as though in the retrospective light of conversion even those who attempted to lead Augustine astray can be seen sympathetically, even charitably. For God was at work in Augustine's attempts to wonder away from him. In fact, all sin, all willful attempt to wander from God, is but a failed effort at independence and distance from him. We cannot but imitate God—the question is whether we will pridefully imitate God's sovereignty to our detriment, or whether we will imitate God's humility in Christ and love for others?

Finally we have in this book a set of fascinating excurses about the body of a saint after death. Augustine celebrates his mother's progress to the point of no longer worrying about where her physical remains will lie—a seeming triumph of the spirit's ascent to God after death at the expense of the body (173). Yet we remember earlier in the book a lovely description of the miraculous discovery of two saints' bodies, and their translation by Ambrose to his basilica (165). The holiness of Gervasius' and Protasius' actual (and physically intact) bodies makes blind people well, one of whom so moves the heretical Empress that she lifts a persecution of the church! (165). We have here a seeming celebration of the goodness of the body, for the bodies of the saints do not even decay, and far from making others unclean, they make them well.[4] This makes us return to Monica's story a second time, where we see that her confidence that the location of her remains matters not is in fact due to a robust belief in the future resurrection of her body, and not to any derogation of the flesh: "'There is no ground for fear that [God] may not acknowledge me at the end of the world and raise me up'" (174). Augustine closes this book by an appeal to us—his readers—to join him in his prayers for his parents at the Lord's altar. It was the common belief of the ancient church that most of the souls of the dead (saints excepted) were still on pilgrimage, and so still in need of our prayers as they journey toward God.

---

[4] See Peter Brown's book, *The Cult of the Saints* (Chicago: University of Chicago, 1981), for more on this fascinating topic. We should say here that Brown's magnificent biography of Augustine, *Augustine of Hippo* (Berkeley: University of California Press, 1967) remains unsurpassed, not only as a scholarly biography, but as great literature in its own right.

For Reflection

- What, finally, do we make of Monica's role in Augustine's life? Who has, for us, cut a similarly imposing figure in our spiritual lives?

- Is it surprising that Augustine can say nice things about heretics—when he is the very one who makes the key arguments for why the imperial authorities should be called in to help the church discipline its enemies?[5]

- What do we make of this complex picture? Souls are clearly valued more deeply here than bodies; yet bodies are in no way disdained. Death is clearly an enemy, one over which Christians celebrate victory as partakers in Christ's resurrection. Yet there is still (mysteriously) work to be done on us after our deaths on the way to God.

- How do any of these views compare with yours and your church's on life after death, body, and soul?[6]

[5] The Donatist schismatics thought the Church Catholic was compromised when its bishops fell during persecution. One should come out and join the Donatist church, led by bishops ordained in a succession without stain. Augustine thought the Donatists located the holiness of baptism in the character of the priest rather than in Christ. He also inveighed upon Rome to use its authority to return Donatists to the Catholic Church forcibly and against their will—setting the stage for all subsequent government enforcement of Christian orthodoxy.

[6] For an eloquent theological defense of these practices see John Bossy, *Christianity in the West 1400–1700* (New York: Oxford University Press, 1987). I've never known so important and thrilling a work to have so boring a title.

Chapter Ten:
BOOK X

THE CONFESSIONS BEGINS HERE to kick into a higher philosophical register than most readers today care to follow. Yet there is every reason to think Augustine thought this portion of the book as important as any that came before, and perhaps more so. If the work began talking less about God, more about Augustine, now it has moved in a proper direction to speaking more about God, and less about Augustine. Writing after the fact about his own work, Augustine described Book X as the pivot of *Confessions*: "The first ten books were written about myself; the last three about Holy Scripture."[1] Like any good preach-

---

[1] The quote is from Augustine's *Retractiones*, in which he revisits his career in letters. It is cited in Pamela Bright, "Book Ten: The Self Seeking the God who Creates and Heals," in *A Reader's Companion to Augustine's Confessions*, ed. Paffenroth and Kennedy. *Retractiones* is a treasure trove for historians, for it allows them to date and situate most of Augustine's works in the larger context of his career—notoriously difficult activities in the case of most historical figures. But the title of that work, *Retractiones*, is a false cognate—it is not *Retractions*. Despite an occasional *mea culpa*, Augustine mostly defends everything he's said and heaps more dirt on his various enemies. The book is available as *St. Augustine: Retractions*, Fathers of the Church (Washington, D.C.: Catholic University of America Press, 1999).

er, Augustine is not only trying to inform us, but to lure us into the very life of God. Early in the work, while reading along about his life, the narration would switch suddenly into prayer—so the reader finds herself, almost unwittingly, praying along.[2] Now Augustine is attempting to usher us, his "fellow citizens and pilgrims" (181) more fully into the sort of intellectual and spiritual ascent toward God that he himself has often experienced and described in this work. If the reading seems tough going, that's no surprise—to attain to the vision of God should not be easy!

Early in this book Augustine makes a confession that sounds innocent (read: boring!) enough when he pronounces his love for the Lord (183). Then he asks a question hard enough to make the confession interesting: "but what am I loving when I love you?" Surely nothing physical, nothing that can be experienced with our bodily senses. "Yet there is a light I love, and a food, and a kind of embrace when I love my God"—notice all five physical senses are included—"a light, voice, odour, food, embrace of my inner man" (183). We might say that for Augustine human apprehension of God is not simply non-physical. It is *like* something we experience with our physical senses, yet God is surely far above anything sensual. Augustine looks around at physical things—they which used to suggest the Manichaeans were right and creation was evil—and they speak poetically to him: "with a great voice they cried out: 'He made us'" (183). The beauty of created things tells him to seek higher, for as good as they are, they are not God, for they change and cause harm and disappoint just as much as they point to their Creator. So he leaves behind the attempt to find God through sense organs, which humans share with beasts, and thinks to "find" God in his memory (185).

---

[2] I owe this observation to Professor Amy Laura Hall (Duke University).

Augustine is impressed with "the vast palaces" of his memory, more so the more he thinks of it. For with it he can summon whatever past sense impression he likes, or whatever future hope he wishes (186–87). It allows one to "see" things not actually now seen (187). All his vast education is stored in his memory (187–88). One can even remember that one has previously remembered something (190), or can recall an emotion without now experiencing it (191). He's interested that one can remember the idea of forgetfulness (193). Playful as he is with the idea of memory, Augustine eventually settles down to serious matters. God has dwelt in Augustine's memory ever since he came to know Him, or even before, since he was prepared for baptism as an infant (13). What Augustine has been *doing* for ten books of *Confessions* now is to search for God in his memory, and to let his readers in on that search. For God has graciously "conferred this honour on my memory" by dwelling in it (200). Yet problems remain—God is no more *physically* in Augustine's memory than he is anywhere else in material creation. Augustine is so impressed with his memory because its ability to contravene time and space is somewhat akin to God's not being limited by those created things. Yet not entirely. Memory fails, and is limited to one person's experiences and ability rightly to remember them. Or, conversely, memory can serve all too well in remembering past sins, such as Augustine's various sexual misdeeds. Memory is then finally an unreliable source for true knowledge of the perfect God. Augustine must then insist to God that "you are not the mind itself" (201). The intellectual search for God in his memory, his mind, fails. Yet of course the effort is not futile, for in searching his memory he can confess, famously, "Late have I loved you, beauty so old and so new: late have I loved you." A memory of life without God can be bewailed. It can also be scoured for signs of the

God who was already pursuing him as Augustine, prodigal-like, fled.

So Augustine turns to the moral sphere in his search for God. He notes an ancient moral truism: that everyone seeks happiness, even if they disagree violently over the meaning of that word (196). Yet the desire for happiness is slippery. If it is unrelated to truth, then the drunkard Augustine once envied is happiest of all, and the powerful imperial rhetor Augustine was then should indeed be pitied. Yet Augustine, now a converted Christian, must confess that happiness is "joy based on the truth," which Truth is God himself (199). Yet as we have seen through Augustine's long and difficult battle with his own will, even after he had some intellectual grasp of the truth, the moral struggle of living as a Christian hardly proved easy! Even once he knows that happiness is joy in the truth, he must still ask God to enable his recalcitrant will to act on that knowledge: "grant what you command, and command what you will" (202).[3]

Augustine spends much of the rest of this book essaying on the ways the intellect and the will can continually be deceived in their twin search for God. The "spiritual senses" can and frequently do lead to sin rather than perception of God (203–10). The three-fold sins of 1 John 2:16 recur—lust of the eyes, vain *curiositas*, and ambition always lurk, attempting to corral human desire back away from God.

---

[3] This lovely line set off a polemical powder keg later in Augustine's career. A British monk named Pelagius heard it quoted by a bishop who was defending Christians' inability to avoid sin. He began to look into Augustine further and discovered what he took to be an abominable moral licentiousness, for surely the claim that one could not avoid sin without divine grace opens the door to all sorts of self-justification. The resulting pamphlet war between Augustine and Pelagius, and Pelagius's clever defender Julian of Eclanum, came to shape western debates about nature and grace and the nature of sin. See the standard biographies for more.

These three sins represent the misuse of good human faculties—for our senses, our intellectual interest, our desire for excellence, are all God-given and good.[4] Yet we twist them into service of ourselves such that they become agents that distance us from God. It seems that for every triumphant step of intellectual and spiritual ascent Augustine makes, there are two temptations to step far backward, ready to assail him. Even when Augustine manages to notice his sin and attempt to correct it, he finds his pride on the increase just so (216–17). The danger is that even a masterful account of the human tendency to self-deception like the *Confessions* can *itself* turn into a source of pride for its author! The word for these crafty vices that can turn would-be virtues into sin is "concupiscence." Sin in the baptized Christian is a tinderbox—it can alight at any moment—and yet it is temporarily defused. Augustine's turn to Jesus at the end of this book is a description of the Great Physician as a healer of concupiscence, who turns these twisted vices back into the virtues for which they were intended.[5]

This is precisely where the *Confessions* shows its greatest genius (or deepest humility?!). A Christian spiritual life is not finally a heroic ascent, fighting off opponents, climbing to a God who's then glad you finally made it. Our way to God is not, despite the impression left by this difficult chapter, a remarkable intellectual feat of climbing from one higher concept of God to another. Rather, in this divine/human encounter, all the "work" is being done from the divine end. Augustine exults that he has good reason to trust in God. Whereas even well-honed spiritual senses, the recogni-

---

[4] I have already cited Paul Griffith's forthcoming book about *curiositas*. This is a particularly curious Augustinian sin—not least his example of it: watching a spider devour flies (213). In our day he might have pointed to watching cable television's ubiquitous nature shows!

[5] I take this point from Pamela Bright's essay cited above.

tion of and attempt to avoid sin, the brilliant search for God in one's mind, above one's mind, through one's desire—all these can and do turn out to be misleading attempts at human *apotheosis*, a grab for spiritual glory and heroic religious accomplishment. In contrast, Christianity teaches a mediator who "ought to have something in common with God and something in common with humanity" (219). Rather than heroic ascent, we have here divine descent, into the very stuff of human life: sight, sound, touch, taste, feel, in such mundane practices as the church's attempt to love each other and seek the truth. Augustine concludes this magnificent book with the prayer of a priest: "'Let not the proud speak evil of me,' for I think upon the price of my redemption, and I eat and drink it, and distribute it.[6] In my poverty I desire to be satisfied from it together with those who 'eat and are satisfied.' 'And they shall praise the Lord who seek him'" (220). Despite our efforts to grasp for God, God is already present among us, in bread, wine, water, word, one another.

For Reflection

- Chart the differing ways in which Augustine uses the word "confession" in the first few pages of this book. Do those paragraphs throw light on the genre of *Confessions* as a whole?

- Can one find God in one's memory? Why or why not?

[6] Clearly a reference to the Eucharist, and perhaps a risky one, as Christians at this time still did not speak openly of the actual practice of baptism and Eucharist—those were guarded secrets opened only when one had undergone catechesis and presented oneself to receive them.

- In one of Augustine's sermons he famously said, "if you understand it, it is not God." That is, it is more theologically faithful to say what God is not than what God is. Can you see the fruit here in the latter chapters of *Confessions* of inquiring after what God is not?

- Why is Augustine so worried about the sin of *curiositas*?

- What makes for genuine human happiness for Augustine? For you?

Chapter Eleven:
BOOK XI

HERE WE SEE AUGUSTINE exploring another philosophically vexing topic: time. In the last book we saw that memory is a created human capacity that resembles divine eternity in its ability to transcend the present, yet at an infinite remove, since memory can err, cause to sin, and finally fails to reach God. All the same, memory is indispensable to the human search for God. So too with time. Time is a knife's edge. As soon as a moment is here, it is gone, another has taken its place. This unending procession of moments is somewhat akin to the eternal "now" in which God "exists," since for God every moment in created time is always already present. Yet the ongoing succession of moments is not eternity, for eternity is not simply unending time, it is qualitatively *different*, in ways we cannot even explain.

As in the last chapter with regard to memory, Augustine will here plumb the depths of time for clues about the divine mystery, yet will come away barely more enlightened than before he began. What mere creature can understand such things? All the same his search will end in praise, for a God who finds him even before he begins searching, who makes possible even the limited intellectual or spiritual discoveries we make, and whose glory is finally the purpose of such explorations as these.

On its surface these seem like questions any pious Platonist could raise: God's difference from creation, the inability of one to reach the other, the incommensurability of time and eternity, and so on. But, of course, these questions are more pressing for a Christian. For we believe not only that time and eternity, creation and Creator are radically distinct, but also that their distinction has been broached in the incarnation of Christ. No Christian, however Platonist, can simply disparage time, since it is now an arena in which God has made an appearance, as it were—a theater of divine glory. The explorations here are not then of the intellectual parlor game variety, nor even the material for debates among philosophy students. They are rather the very stuff of Christian reflection on salvation, the God who saves, and the nature of us creatures who are on salvation's receiving-end.

The explorations include not a few false starts. What was God doing before creation? If we cannot allow the defensive surliness of the insecure Sunday School teacher, "preparing hells for people who inquire into profundities," then what should we say (229)? The answer is easy enough: there was no "was" before God created time. Yet Augustine cannot help thinking a bit harder about the nature of time and its relationship to the eternity that God is. Time and eternity are not simply opposed to one another, even if they are inescapably different. The to-and-fro of time somehow reflects timeless eternity, since all that comes and goes in time does so for some mysterious reason in the eternal Reason of God (226). To state this positive view of time a bit more strongly, time is the condition of the possibility of human relationship to divine eternity. He uses the example of the recitation of a song or poem: "What occurs in the psalm as a whole occurs in its particular pieces and its individual syllables. The same is true of a longer action in which the psalm is a part. It is also valid of the entire life of an individual person, where all actions are parts of a whole, and of the whole history of the 'sons of men' where all human lives are but parts" (243). Time and eternity are not to be opposed to one another as antagonists, but the former is to be seen as a participant in the latter, allowing creatures in time the chance to take part in eternity. Just as God is high above creatures—eternal, almighty, all wise—and this greatness is no barrier to involvement in human life through divine speech, calling, incarnation, so divine eternity is no artificial barrier to God's participation in temporal human life. It is rather the condition of the possibility of divine involvement in human life without loss to either. Eternity is the divine "distance" that allows creatures to grow toward the divine unendingly.

Augustine here "plays" with the notion of time as he did before with that of memory. How can God not change, and creation not be eternal (228)? His faith requires him to believe both, yet their coexistence is mysterious, seemingly paradoxical. Augustine muses that only if he is asked what time is does he seem suddenly not to know (230)! Time only exists as it is passing away, so there cannot really be a "time" of long duration—it is simply an infinite collection of nanoseconds that will not sit still even to be measured (231–32). If the future and the past exist, they do so only *as present*, so if we speak of three "times," they are the presence of the past, the presence of the present, and the presence of the future (233–34).

Augustine puzzles over the demonic success of fortune-tellers and the angelic version of prophets—how do both seem to have some purchase on the divine purview of the future? And he burns to solve these mysteries, as a way toward the God he loves (236). Augustine's wonderings here are not an opening to despair, but marvelings in the face of a mystery. We cannot comprehend divine creation, the bringing about of all that is from nothing—no human act of making can even offer an analogy to such an "event." But because God can enter into history without loss to himself or creation's integrity, we can infer that creation is both distinct from God and indicative of God's goodness. If Platonist philosophy is the raw material of such questions as time and eternity, Christian Trinitarian and Christological thought are the anvil on which this doctrine of creation is being hammered.

We could continue in great detail to explore Augustine's thought in this book. Yet we will conclude with his concluding note—"let the person who understands this make confession to you. Let him who fails to understand it make confession to you" (245). The distinction between time and eternity that marks creatures and God is no barrier, keeping God from his creatures. In fact, since God is able to be immediately present to any moment in created time, it is a short step from creation to incarnation. For the very "beginning" in which God created according to Genesis 1:1 is none other than Christ (226). Yet Augustine does want to make clear that exploration of these themes is no easy intellectual task. In polemical works, he often makes a rhetorical move I call "thickening the mystery." For example, in response to critics who ask how Christ can have been both human and divine, Augustine will not explain the two natures, but will ask something like, "can you explain how your body and soul join together?" The echo of Jesus' "then I will not answer your question either," is not accidental. The world is shot through with mystery, not only in the most "religious" places, but in the mundane, down to the passing seconds which are the stream in which we swim.

Augustine wishes to make sure our portions of the stream flow back to their divine source.[1]

For Reflection

* What is time?

* What do you think of when you hear God described as "transcendent"? Does the word connote distance—God hovering afar off? Does it suggest closeness, God closer than you are to yourself? How does this chapter inform your answer?

* Among the vast array of metaphors for salvation in *Confessions*, one of the most striking is that of Augustine's scattered self, and God's work of gathering those pieces together. What does salvation look like when viewed through that particular prism?

---

[1] This metaphor of "flowing" is rightly emphasized in Robert Kennedy, "Book Eleven: The *Confessions* as Eschatological Narrative," in *A Reader's Companion to Augustine's Confessions,* ed. Paffenroth and Kennedy, 167–84. It is also highlighted in interesting ways in Miroslav Volf's new book, *Free of Charge: Giving and Forgiving in a Culture Stripped of Grace* (Grand Rapids: Zondervan, 2006).

Chapter Twelve:
BOOKS XII–XIII

A UGUSTINE OPENS THESE BOOKS with a worry about the relationship between wordiness and pride (247), and openly wonders whether we, his readers, can follow his explorations of such abstract concepts as immaterial existence (248). Many readers have indeed found him wordy and themselves uninterested in doing the work to follow along here. Yet we can take Augustine's own marveling at the scriptures and apply them, not inappropriately, to our reading of Augustine's own works. He speaks to God: "What wonderful profundity there is in your utterances! The surface meaning lies open before us and charms beginners. Yet the depth is amazing, my God, the depth is amazing" (254). Some readers of *Confessions* may be satisfied with the salacious details of Augustine's early life and his conversion in Book VIII. Others will want to wade more deeply into the depths of these later books, there to watch a master intellect and spirit at work, and so to be shaped in mind and spirit after his image, as his is shaped after the image of Christ (1 Corinthians 11:1).

These final books have a hidden polemical subtext to which Augustine does not actually alert us. At the time of his writing he was doing battle with a heretical group in

North Africa known as the Donatists. The origin of this debate was in persecutions of the church in the early 4th century. Under threat of torture and death, some Christian priests and bishops either recanted their faith or surrendered copies of the gospels. After the lifting of persecution and the offering of imperial favor to the church, the question became what to do with these lapsed church leaders? And not only that—but what to do about the sacraments they had administered? For example, if I were married or baptized by a cleric who later apostasized, is my baptism or marriage valid? After all, if he could surrender his faith under mere threat of external harm, could he ever really have been holy at all—and so able to distribute holiness to others?

Augustine responded with an emphatic "yes." Even a lapsed priest is still a priest, since the holiness he distributes is not his at all, but rather Christ's. The efficacy of the sacrament depends then not on the goodness of the one administering but on the power of God, working through this human agent. Augustine saw not only the social upheaval that could result from nullification of sacraments after the fact, but also the cult of personality that could grow up around clerics' holiness if their sacramental ministries depended on their own personal holiness (or lack thereof). Naturally, his Donatist enemies replied that he was opening the way for laxity. A likely course of action—since Augustine himself was once an avowed heretic! "Maybe he still is," his detractors whispered. Not a few scholars pinpoint the particular historical rationale for the penning of the *Confessions* on Augustine's need to explain himself as a new bishop to his flock. They did not know him personally, he had been off in Italy or wherever. If they did know him it was to his detriment—as a prominent Manichaean heretic. This is why Augustine is so keen to identify his teaching with the work of the Holy Spirit in this book (250). It is also a possible reason for the extraordinary marriage between biblical exploration and passionate religious fervor expressed in these pages. It is as though Augustine needs to show that being a Catholic is not less a reason for zeal than being a Donatist— in fact, it is more so. For it involves the relentless pursuit of Christ, recognition of the dogged persistence of sin, and attempts to overcome it through prayer and reading of the scriptures. Clearly Donatists have no monopoly on serious pursuit of discipline.[1]

It is not inappropriate then to begin with Augustine's reflections on scripture in these final two books. Augustine concludes his autobiography with nothing less than biblical interpretation. It is as though he means to say that the goal of human memory, reason, and will should finally be the search for divine glory in the pages of scripture. It is also as though he wishes to say that God may be found much more reliably in the pages of scripture than in the memoirs of Augustine's own life. Yet scripture is difficult. He himself had been put off by it as a young man, and so became a Manichaean, since they seemed better able to account for the moral oddities of the bible. Later, as a young convert, Augustine had been unable to make heads or tails of the book of Isaiah, despite Ambrose's recommendation of it. Augustine finally came to realize that scripture's odd loose ends and moral quagmires—the immoralities of the patriarchs, the quasi-physical and anthropomorphic depiction of God, and the general barbarity of its language in comparison to graceful Cicero—could be reconciled to a Christian intelligence through *allegorical* exegesis. That is, by offering "another reading" than that seemingly called for by the letter. So, the "beginning" in which God creates in Genesis cannot suggest temporality before creation

---

[1] This last paragraph is dependent on Thomas Martin, O.S.A., "Book Twelve: Exegesis and *Confessio*," in *A Reader's Companion to Augustine's Confessions,* ed. Paffenroth and Kennedy, 185–206.

(the patent meaning of the letter), and so must be taken to mean Christ. All things then can properly be seen as created through Christ, whose descent in incarnation and cross are then seen as not antithetical to creation (so the Manichaeans), but the fulfillment of God's original purpose in creation. We might say that *Confessions* itself is a work of biblical exegesis, showing not only what the words of the bible "mean," but also presenting Augustine's own life as a sort of "reading" of the bible for others to emulate.

Augustine even makes the strikingly post-modern sounding claim here that the attainment to whatever was in Moses' head as he wrote the Pentateuch is merely a distraction to the search for biblical meaning!

> See now how stupid it is, among so large a mass of entirely correct interpretations which can be elicited from those words, rashly to assert that a particular one has the best claim to be Moses' view, and by destructive disputes to offend against charity itself, which is the principle of everything he said in the texts we are attempting to expound. (265)

Augustine always already knows what a biblical text is going to "mean" before he reads it—it is going to refer to the triune God and to further its readers' pursuit of love of God and neighbor. The "game" of exegesis then is to see how these particular words bear witness to that meaning (in short, to the creed). So Moses' words in Genesis here can be put to uses that may have shocked Moses (and do shock modern Old Testament scholars, and perhaps not a few of us!). But the way of reading makes perfect sense to Augustine. For him the question is how precisely to find Christ's saving presence in these words, and just so, how to improve his readers' love of God and neighbor?[2] Furthermore, disagreement among friends in pursuing a text's "meaning" is intrinsic to God's saving work among us. As Augustine writes elsewhere, "there would be no way for love, which ties people together in bonds of unity, to make souls overflow and as it were intermingle with each other, if human beings learned nothing from other humans."[3] Like rabbis disputing the meaning of a Talmudic reading of the Torah, Christians pore over the text of scripture together with the help of such fathers as Augustine. In our disagreements with one another and the saints we come to love one another and the saints—all through the words of scripture.

It is also no accident that Augustine concludes with a treatment of the created order. Throughout his life he has sought God, or at least his own happiness, which he eventually came to see as only viably locatable in God. He has long sought the right way to look for God through created things. Do creation's vicissitudes and palpable evil suggest a cosmic war in the heavens in which God is, if not losing, at least taking casualties? (so the Manichaeans). Or is God to be identified as radically distinct from this world, so that physical things are mere replicas of true things "located" "elsewhere" (indeed, when would one stop using scare quotes with a truly Platonist system?). Or, is evil to be explained as non-being, material vicissitude as the possibility for growth in God, and the divine as a benevolent creator who stoops anew to meet us in Christ and is now slowly gathering all humanity to himself in the power of the Spirit through the church? This last, Catholic view wins of

[2] For more on Augustine's biblical hermeneutics and a defense of such practices today, see Robert Wilken's *The Spirit of Early Christian Thought: Seeking the Face of God* (New Haven: Yale University Press, 2003).

[3] In his *On Christian Teaching*, trans. R. P. H. Green, The World's Classics (Oxford: Oxford University Press, 1997).

course, and now Augustine turns to review creation again, to account both for its flaws and its glories, in a properly Christian light.

Creation is not part of God, for how could God have parts? And if creation were God, shouldn't we worship it (249)? Further, Christian belief in God as Trinity suggests God had no *need* of creation, since he suffered no lack in his own fullness of fellowship (275). Creation is then a gratuitous, free expression of divine love. There is no need for it, yet it is there, as an object of divine delight. Further, creation is the theater of the divine glory, the arena in which God himself has manifested his glory, in Israel, in Jesus, in Church. Human attempts humbly to love one another in the church are proper reflections of a God who as Trinity is always mutually-outpouring love, who in creation and redemption pours himself out to that which is not-God: creatures. The "point" of all life is then the church—in its halting, stumbling attempts to love, to be trained out of sin and into virtue, its efforts at *wise charity* (1 Corinthians 1:24; Romans 5:5) among its members—this is a dim, but real, reflection of the divine triunity.

Finally we must say a final word about Augustine himself. He spent much of this book as a restless figure, seeking rest in God, first without knowing it, then despite poor knowledge of God, then with true knowledge but a recalcitrant will, and now finally with full heart and mind in the church. We might say Augustine only "finds himself" as he loses himself more deeply and spectacularly in the divine mystery. The ornate and mystical final books of *Confessions* are far from antithetical to Augustine's autobiographical purposes. It is as though he is saying, 'to know me, gaze upon God; in fact to know yourself do the same.' Creation, including us, has no *being* in itself, it has being only in God, so to find ourselves aright we must find God aright, and lose ourselves in him (249). To shift the image slightly, Augustine has often reflected on his nature as a "scattered" self, being "gathered" only by divine action. Yet he is not "gathered" in some stable way to take possession of himself, he is "gathered" only as it were "upward," directed toward God, still in fragments, since his "whole" self is only in a God who cannot be located, but only grown-toward (278). Ironically, this "flight" toward himself and the divine simultaneously does not mean a withdrawal from the hard realities of this world, though he is tempted toward that at Cassiciacum (Book IX). Rather, this flight demands a greater engagement with the humble particularity of his flock at Hippo, to whom this book may have been intended as an introduction of Augustine as their new preacher (221).[4] The way to "ascend" to this God is to "descend," to the humble realities of church life, boring committee meetings, ornery fellow human beings, with weak commitments and half-baked intentions, the very grime and glory of life. *That* people is our means to growth into *this* God. Not a solo intellectual flight, but a descent to the crucified God at our feet, and the humble, stubborn, intractable people at the church you grew up in.

For Reflection

- Examples of allegory abound in these books' interpretation of Genesis 1–3—as popular a topic as there is in ancient Christian exegesis with its treatment of creation. Is Augustine's way of interpreting scripture palatable in our day? Why or why not?[5]

[4] Peter Brown's suggestion of the purpose of *Confessions*; see his *The Body and Society: Men, Women, and Sexual Renunciation in Early Christianity* (New York: Columbia University Press, 1988).

[5] There has been extraordinary work done in the last half generation on allegory. See, above all, the stirring article by David Steinmetz, "The Superiority of Pre-Critical Exegesis," in *The Theological Interpretation*

* How does the holiness of the saints affect the way we read scripture? Put differently—will you ever be able to read Romans 13:13-14 without thinking of Au-gustine's conversion?!

* How do Augustine's musings here on creation as a reflection of the divine Trinity show that trinitarian thought—often assigned to the dusty basement of useless Christian esoterica and useless thought— might actually be helpful for tangible moral and spiritual questions in our lives?

* How do his thoughts on the theological significance of creation suggest we ought to take care of the natural order, of our bodies, of one another?

* What are the major issues you disagree with Augustine about?

* How are Augustine's life and work an example for yours?

* Has Augustine helped you see your life with new eyes? To recommit yourself to Christ, to the church, and so to yourself?

of Scripture: Classic and Contemporary Readings, ed. Steven Fowl (Oxford: Blackwell, 1997) 26–38.

GLOSSARY

1. People[1]

Adeodatus (372–389). The son Augustine fathered with his unnamed concubine. The boy showed exceptional intellectual promise, and was Augustine's dialogue partner in his *On the Teacher,* available in the *Ancient Christian Writers* series, vol. 9 (New York: Newman, 1950). Augustine recalls his life and death briefly, but proudly, almost as a prelude to talk of their baptism together by Ambrose (Chadwick, 163–64).

Alypius. Augustine's lifelong friend (98), whom he first led to the Manicheans (100), then who converted to catholic Christianity immediately after Augustine did (153), and later became Bishop of Thagaste in North Africa.

[1] For background and dates I have extensively used Allan Fitzgerald, OSA, editor, *Augustine through the Ages: An Encyclopedia* (Grand Rapids: Eerdmans, 1999); F. L. Cross and E. A. Livingstone, editors, *The Oxford Dictionary of the Christian Church*, 3d ed. (Oxford: Oxford University Press, 1997); and the footnotes in Henry Chadwick's translation of *Confessions*, The World's Classics (Oxford: Oxford University Press, 1998).

Ambrose (ca. 339–397). Along with Augustine one of the four great "doctors" (or "teachers") of the western church. His rhetorical fame led Augustine to listen to his preaching (87). His defense of the Old Testament and demonstration of allegorical exegesis as part of the pursuit of wisdom attracted him (95). The two seem not to have been close personally (92), though Ambrose did baptize Augustine (164).

Anselm (1033–1109). A major theological figure in the medieval church who furthered Augustine's thought in a new time and idiom. His most famous works offer what's been called the "ontological argument" for God's existence (in the *Proslogion*) and a defense of the incarnation and atoning work of Jesus ("Why God Became Man"), both available in *Anselm of Canterbury: The Major Works,* The World's Classics (New York: Oxford University Press, 1998).

Anthony (251–356). Often called the founder of monasticism, Anthony fled the easy Christianity of his youth to pray and struggle with demons in the desert. Augustine hears his story from Ponticianus and is inspired to think that ascetic renunciation of prestige and sex is not only possible, but desirable (142). St. Athanasius immortalized his life and teaching with his *Life of Antony*, available as part of the Classics of Western Spirituality series (New York: Paulist, 1980).

Augustine (354–430). Western Christianity's most formative post-biblical thinker on such topics as creation and fall, the church and the sacraments, sin and grace. He is also Western Christianity's most famous convert due to his magnificent *Confessions*.

Cicero (106–43 BC). A philosopher, orator, and statesman, he was a key figure in translating and spreading Hellenistic philosophy into the Latin world. A key figure in Augustine's conversion to philosophy, whose work actually changed Augustine's "feelings" (39). A key resource throughout Augustine's intellectual life: he uses him in his own work on rhetoric in *On Christian Teaching* (Oxford: The World's Classics, 1997) and argues with him about politics in the famous book 19 of the *City of God* (Cambridge: Cambridge University Press, 1998).

Faustus. A Manichean bishop with a reputation for erudition, Augustine eagerly awaited a meeting with him to clear up some of his doubts about Manichean belief. He found him personally amiable enough (77), but sub-par in his learning (78), in stark contrast to Ambrose, whose erudition and piety helped bring about Augustine's final conversion.

Jerome (345–420). Another of the four great doctors of the western church (the fourth was Pope Gregory the Great), he was a great ascetic and theologian and an extraordinarily important linguist, whose translation of the Old Testament directly from Hebrew into Latin (bypassing the Greek Septuagint), the Vulgate, served the Catholic church for more than a millennium. Augustine relied on his knowledge of Hebrew and famously sparred with him for tinkering with old Latin translations of the scriptures that were beloved by church people, but often inaccurate.

Julian of Eclanum (380–454). Son of a bishop, of refined cultural upbringing, and a dogged opponent of Augustine late in his life. His defense of free will and criticisms of Augustine's doctrine of original sin included the suggestion that Augustine never really got over his Manichean past.

Mani (ca. 216–277). His teaching derived from Gnostic sources in his native Persia; he taught there and in India before being put to death by a Persian king, after which his teaching spread to north Africa and Rome. He taught a rigid dualism between light and dark, in which a cosmic war between the two resulted in the creation of the base material world with particles of light trapped in darkness, needing to be freed by certain practices of the Manichean "elect." The young Augustine found they had better explanations for natural phenomena than did the unlearned Catholics he knew.

Marius Victorinus (ca 290–?). "Victorinus!" "Victorinus!" The thrilled whispers whistled through the crowded church in which the converted Platonist philosopher made his profession of faith. That Victorinus could make such a conversion suggested to Augustine he could too— and likewise that he could turn his prodigious rhetorical ability to the service of the church. Victorinus' work on the Trinity was some of the most influential in the western church (135–40).

Monica (c. 331–387). Augustine's mother is the most vivid character in *Confessions*—perhaps more textured than Augustine himself! Her piety allows her son to drink in Jesus' name with her milk. Her worry over him threatens to drive him away both from faith and from her. Her prayers and tears, by one bishop's account, guarantee his conversion (51). Her habits of piety suggest the backwardness of north African Catholicism that repelled her son once—yet she can recognize Ambrose's genius and saintliness (91). And she and her son enjoy a final glimpse of the beatific vision together before her death (171).

Nebridius (d. ca. 391). Close childhood friend of Augustine's, ventured with him to Milan, and then back to north Africa to participate with him in their quasi-monastic community's search for wisdom. A persistent religious seeker before his conversion, his questions were clearly salutary to Augustine's own searching.

Patrick (d. 370–371). Augustine's father was a minor government official in their hometown of Thagaste. His self-seeking in promoting Augustine's education, and in his excitement over Augustine's sexual maturity, are the only shadows his distant memory casts over *Confessions*. His late-life conversion is attributed to Monica's influence over her husband (170).

Pelagius. This British monk was aghast at Augustine's teaching on original sin, thinking such prayers as "Grant what you command, and command what you will" undercut human freedom and any incentive for people to take steps toward God for themselves (202). Under goading from him and from Julian of Eclanum, Augustine formulated his mature teaching on sin and grace, freedom and providence, that have been crucial in all subsequent western Christianity.

Ponticianus. A fellow African and court official in Milan who, visiting Augustine and Alypius one day, notices their volume of the epistles of Paul. He announces he too is a Christian, and proceeds to tell them of St. Anthony, of whom they had not previously heard. This and further ascetic examples of converts breaking off engagements to pursue ascetic lives help inspire Augustine's conversion (and so of many thousands in his train).

Possidius (370–440). Augustine's biographer, his friend of many years, participant with him in one of his monastic communities, later bishop of Calama, some forty miles from Hippo. His portrait of Augustine has him, above all, as a churchman—a preacher and administrator.

2. Terms

Allegory. A practice of reading a text in some "other sense" than what is conventional. Christians followed forebears both pagan and Jewish in reading scripture with reference to Christian teaching. Augustine found Ambrose's allegorical readings of the Old Testament especially helpful for giving him a way to understand what he took to be literally inelegant texts as mysteries pointing toward Christ.

Asceticism. A set of practices dedicating to disciplining the body and shaping desire such that it seek satisfaction in God and right love of neighbor. Augustine's hearing of St. Anthony's and others' ascetic practice was a key to his own conversion. Later he initiated efforts at ascetic communal living for those who have not retreated into the desert, first with friends and family at Cassiciacum, and later with his priests at Hippo.

Cassiciacum. The country estate of the Milanese rhetorician Verecundus to which Augustine and friends retreated after his conversion and before his baptism. Their primary goal there was to seek wisdom through philosophical conversation. Augustine also wrote some of his first treatises there.

Curiositas. One of the triumvirate of sins described in 1 John 2:16. Augustine takes it to mean inordinate attention to a created thing at the expense of its creator. The word has drifted and now means something different from our own word "curiosity," which we take to be an intellectual virtue. Augustine lauds and practices studiousness and wonder in pursuit of new learning about God and God's world, even as he criticizes interest in something for its own sake without reference to God.[2]

Donatism. Theological controversy in north Africa resulting from the problem of what the church ought to do with those who lapsed during persecution. When one of Rome's periodic persecutions of the early church broke out, some bishops and priests would "apostasize" (renounce their faith), or turn over copies of Bibles to authorities. After persecutions lifted, Christians divided over whether these priests' sacraments had been valid. The Donatists were those who held that only sacraments performed by priests who never renounced their faith were valid—others must be re-baptized. Augustine's position, carved out over against the Donatists, won the day and has held sway in the western church since: the validity of the sacrament depends on the holiness of Christ, and not of the celebrant. Augustine also mocked the Donatists for suggesting the church catholic was limited to a few holdouts for holiness in backwater places in north Africa, whereas the mixed church of sinners and sacred is worldwide ("catholic").

Exegesis. Literally the "drawing out" of meaning from a text. Exegesis of the Bible especially is a crucial activity for priests writing sermons, theologians writing about God,

---

[2] See Paul Griffiths, "The Vice of Curiosity," *Pro Ecclesia* 15 (2006) 47–63.

the church teaching converts, and any number of other religious tasks.

Hippo Regius. The small town that saw a rising star in young Augustine and ordained him its bishop before a bigger, more prestigious town could claim him. As Augustine lay dying it was surrounded by invading Vandals. Now Bône in eastern Algeria.

Hermeneutics. Principles of interpretation by which one does "exegesis." For example, to interpret the word "Zion" as a reference to heaven is an act of exegesis. The theology that leads one to conclude that Old Testament place names like Zion are meant to refer to Christian theological concepts like heaven makes up one's "hermeneutics."

Manicheanism. Religion the early Augustine found quite attractive, pursuing it as a "hearer" for a decade. Its origins are in the teachings of Mani, a third-century Persian, who held that the origins of this evil material world are in a great cosmic battle between light and dark. The dark succeeded in capturing particles of light, but the Manichean elect or saints can liberate these particles through certain ritual acts of eating certain foods. Augustine came to think it inadequately explained observable phenomena and philosophical truth, and soon after his disenchantment found his way back to the catholic church.

Platonism. System of philosophical beliefs originating with Plato's dialogues, developing with the more elaborate metaphysical speculation of Plotinus and Porphyry. Its signal teachings include a division between matter and the immaterial with the latter more highly regarded than the former—though this is not as stark as with the Gnostics. Material things do offer clues to their participation in eternal things, which the philosopher can see and attempt to teach to others. This wisdom may prove dangerous to him, however, as the mass of people have no interest in immaterial and eternal truth. Early Christians found these teachings helpful for interpreting their biblical texts on such crucial topics as creation and the nature of God.

SELECT
BIBLIOGRAPHY

Augustine. *Confessions*. Translated by Henry Chadwick. The World's Classics. Oxford: Oxford University Press, 1992.

Ayres, Lewis. *Nicaea and Its Legacy: An Approach to Fourth-Century Trinitarian Theology*. Oxford: Oxford University Press, 2004.

Bossy, John. *Christianity in the West 1400–1700*. New York: Oxford University Press, 1987.

Brown, Peter. *Augustine of Hippo: A Biography*. Berkeley: University of California, 2000.

———. *The Body and Society: Men, Women, and Sexual Renunciation in Early Christianity*. New York: Columbia University Press, 1988.

———. *The Cult of the Saints*. Chicago: University of Chicago, 1981.

Buechner, Frederick. *Telling Secrets*. San Francisco: Harper, 1991.

Burnaby, John. *Amor Dei: A Study of the Religion of St. Augustine*. London: Hodder & Stoughton, 1938.

Byassee, Jason. Review of *Augustine: A New Biography* by James J. O'Donnell. *Books and Culture* 2.3 (Sept/Oct 2005) 43–44.

———. *Praise Seeking Understanding*. Grand Rapids: Eerdmans, forthcoming.

Chadwick, Henry. *Augustine: A Very Short Introduction*. New York: Oxford University Press, 2001.

Clement, Olivier. *The Roots of Christian Mysticism*. Hyde Park, N.Y.: New City, 1996.

Dodaro, Robert, and George Lawless, editors. *Augustine and His Critics*. London: Routledge, 2000.

Fitzgerald, Allan D., OSA. *Augustine through the Ages: An Encyclopedia*. Grand Rapids: Eerdmans, 1999.

Fredriksen, Paula. "Paul and Augustine: Conversion Narratives, Orthodox Traditions, and the Retrospective Self." *Journal of Theological Studies* 37 (1986) 3–34.

Hanby, Michael. *Augustine and Modernity*. New York: Routledge, 2003.

Harmless, William. *Augustine and the Catechumenate*. Collegeville, Minn.: Liturgical, 1995.

Harrison, Carol. *Augustine: Christian Truth and Fractured Humanity*. Oxford: Oxford University Press, 2000.

Hart, David. *The Beauty of the Infinite*. Grand Rapids: Eerdmans, 2003.

Jenson, Robert. *Systematic Theology*. 2 vols. New York: Oxford University Press, 1997, 1999.

Lancel, Serge. *St. Augustine*. Translated by Antonia Nevill. London: SCM, 2002.

Lash, Nicholas. *The Beginning and the End of Religion*. Cambridge: Cambridge University Press, 1996.

McGinn, Bernard. *The Presence of God: A History of Western Christian Mysticism*. 4 vols. New York: Crossroad, 1994, 1996, 1998, 2005.

Markus, Robert. *The End of Ancient Christianity*. Cambridge: Cambridge University Press, 1990.

Milbank, John. *Being Reconciled*. London: Routledge, 2003.

———. *Theology and Social Theory*. Oxford: Blackwell, 1990,

———. *The Word Made Strange*. Oxford: Blackwell, 1997.

O'Donnell, James J. *Augustine: Confessions*. 3 vols. Oxford: Clarendon, 1992.

———. *Augustine: A New Biography*. New York: HarperCollins, 2005.

O'Donovan, Oliver. *The Problem of Self-Love in St. Augustine*. New Haven: Yale University Press, 1980.

Paffenroth, Kim, and Robert Kennedy, editors. *A Reader's Companion to Augustine's Confessions*. Louisville: Westminster John Knox, 2003.

Polkinghorne, John. *Exploring Reality: The Intertwining of Science and Religion*. New Haven: Yale University Press, 2006.

Rist, John. *Augustine.* Cambridge: Cambridge University Press, 1994.

Starnes, Colin. *Augustine's Conversion: A Guide to the Argument of Confessions I–IX.* Waterloo, Ont.: Wilfred Laurier University Press, 1991.

Steinmetz, David. "The Superiority of Pre-Critical Exegesis." In *The Theological Interpretation of Scripture: Classic and Contemporary Readings,* edited by Steven Fowl, 26–38. Oxford: Blackwell, 1997.

Stock, Brian. *Augustine the Reader: Meditation, Self-Knowledge, and the Ethics of Interpretation.* Cambridge: Harvard University Press, 1996.

Taylor, Charles. *Sources of the Self: The Making of Modern Identity.* Cambridge: Harvard University Press, 1989.

Volf, Miroslav. *Free of Charge: Giving and Forgiving in a Culture Stripped of Grace.* Grand Rapids: Zondervan, 2006.

Williams, Rowan. *Lost Icons.* Edinburgh: T. & T. Clark, 2000.

Wills, Garry. *Saint Augustine.* Penguin Lives. New York: Viking, 1999.